The Anxiety Field Guide

Healthy Habits for Long-Term Healing

Jason Cusick

An imprint of InterVarsity Press
Downers Grove, Illinois

InterVarsity Press
P.O. Box 1400, Downers Grove, IL 60515-1426
ivpress.com
email@ivpress.com

InterVarsity Press® is the book-publishing division of InterVarsity Christian Fellowship/USA®, a movement of students and faculty active on campus at hundreds of universities, colleges, and schools of nursing in the United States of America, and a member movement of the International Fellowship of Evangelical Students. For information about local and regional activities, visit intervarsity.org.

Unless otherwise indicated, all Scripture quotations are taken from the Holy Bible, New Living Translation, copyright ©1996, 2004, 2007, 2013. Used by permission of Tyndale House Publishers, Inc., Carol Stream, Illinois 60188. All rights reserved.

While any stories in this book are true, some names and identifying information may have been changed to protect the privacy of individuals.

Figure 19.1 from Gloria Wilcox, Feelings: Converting Negatives to Positives *(Augusta: Morris Publishing, 2001).*

Icons by Katrina Chen, used with permission.

The publisher cannot verify the accuracy or functionality of website URLs used in this book beyond the date of publication.

Cover design and image composite: David Fassett
Interior design: Jeanna Wiggins
Image: abstract misty mountain range: © anand purohit / Moment / Getty Images

ISBN 978-1-5140-0345-9 (print)
ISBN 978-1-5140-0346-6 (digital)

Printed in the United States of America ♾

Library of Congress Cataloging-in-Publication Data
A catalog record for this book is available from the Library of Congress.

P	25	24	23	22	21	20	19	18	17	16	15	14	13	12	11	10	9	8	7	6	5	4	3	2	1

Y	40	39	38	37	36	35	34	33	32	31	30	29	28	27	26	25	24	23	22

**To Juanita, Beth, Wayne, Judy,
Angela, Clifford, and Chris**

Thank you for the many ways you've

listened to and counseled me

in my times of anxiety.

To Scott Symington

Thank you for helping me keep my eyes

on the front screen and giving me the skills

to know what to do with the side screen.

To Journey of Faith

Thank you for your encouragement

and patience as I grow in becoming

a nonanxious leader.

*Even when I walk
through the darkest valley,
I will not be afraid,
for you are close beside me.*

PSALM 23:4

Contents

Introduction

I'VE STRUGGLED WITH ANXIETY my whole life. I just didn't know it.

I was raised in a loving and stable home, but my mom was a self-professed "clean freak." Our home was always orderly and well managed. She kept a strict schedule for when and how things should be done. She had a day-planner with all our meals for the month. All our possessions had their place. She recently told me a story of when I was six years old and playing with my toys on the floor. I got up to go to the bathroom and said to her, "Please don't clean up my toys. I'm just going potty."

My mom was never diagnosed with obsessive-compulsive disorder (OCD), but she was always checking things—multiple times. She was never convinced that the front door was locked, the refrigerator closed, or the oven off. It was not unusual for my brother and me to wait for my mom while she checked something for the seventh or eighth time.

She was also a people pleaser. Her mother taught her to be overly concerned about people's opinions of her. She once told me about a conversation she had with her own mom after coming home from the first day at school. She told her mom what people she had met, what her teacher looked like, what she had for lunch, and what she'd learned. Her mom responded by asking, "But did they like you?"

I love my mom. She is caring, thoughtful, funny, self-aware, and strong. I can't think of anyone I'd rather be more like than her. In fact,

I am a lot like her. From my childhood, I was never taught to be anxious. I believe I "caught it" growing up, perhaps through genetics and certainly through my upbringing. I struggled with anxiety but never had words for it. I did have behaviors, though.

From an early age, I was a cheek biter (my own cheeks, not other people's). I would bite my lips and the inside of my mouth when I was stressed out. It was a painful habit. It also gave me mouth sores. One time in high school, I bit up my mouth so badly that I couldn't talk for a day because of the swelling. Only later did I realize that this is clinically called *morsicatio buccarum*, a body-focused repetitive behavior and a possible sign of obsessive-compulsive disorder.

I was also an entertainer. I was praised and rewarded for this. I excelled in performing and was the captain of the speech and debate teams at school. I have a natural gift for this, but I also learned at a young age that making people laugh was an easy way to get people to like me and navigate the awkward world of social cues and relationships.

My dad died when I was eleven years old. He had spent two years in treatment for chronic myelogenous leukemia. I was told he was the thirty-sixth person in the world to receive the then-experimental treatment called a bone marrow transplant. His death rocked our small family and threw me into a world that felt unsafe, unpredictable, and uncertain. I was lonely and sad. I looked for ways to soothe myself, but like my cheek biting, my self-soothing rituals ended up harming me more than helping me.

Like many people with underlying personal struggles, I felt drawn to care for others. After a profound spiritual experience in college, I became a follower of Jesus and went through training to be a hospital chaplain. For almost a decade I walked alongside hurting people facing hardship, uncertainty, and grief. My call to care for others then led me to a local church congregation, where I served in different pastoral leadership roles. In 2013 I was asked to consider the primary leadership role in the church, following the retirement of the senior pastor. This began a stretch of several years that was both exhilarating and devastating.

In 2015 I accepted the position of lead pastor at Journey of Faith, a large and vibrant church in Southern California. While the church thrived in those first two years, I was just surviving. The increase in responsibility triggered new areas of chronic worry and awakened my ungrieved losses, habitual people pleasing, and paralyzing perfectionism.

Outwardly, I was soaring.

Inwardly, I was drowning.

I was flooded with anxiety. I had panic attacks and insomnia. I gained twenty pounds. I was timing my cheek biting so I could still speak on Sundays. It all reached a tipping point when I found myself working on a sermon late into the night. I had been writing, deleting, and rewriting my words for sixteen hours straight because the words just "didn't feel right." In the morning I called my best friend and told him that I thought I had made a mistake by accepting the job. I believed not only was I not helping anyone, but I could be harming people. Then I said, "Maybe the church . . . and my family would be better off without me."

Whoa! Where did that come from?

My friend and I immediately realized that something else was going on. I needed help. Through a few professional connections I had, I found a therapist who specialized in anxiety disorders and also worked with executive-level leaders. Within a few appointments I realized that I was struggling with a form of anxiety and OCD called "purely obsessional" or "Pure O." My ritualized behavior wasn't hoarding, handwashing, or counting, it was "ruminating." Thinking, processing, and reflecting (which were praised and valued skills of my personal and professional development) had morphed into compulsive behaviors that were killing me—mind, body, and spirit.

I spent the next six months learning about anxiety—and myself.

I realized I wasn't a perfectionist. Perfectionism sounds so noble, so virtuous. I was an obsessionist. I was addicted to assurance, intolerant to uncertainty, imbalanced in my mind-body relationship. I couldn't get God to just "fix me" so I'd be better.

I also thought I was the only one struggling with anxiety. But I was wrong.

We All Have Anxiety

We all have anxiety. Anxiety is our automatic response to a perceived threat. We're on a first date, we have a big assignment at work or school, we're walking in a dark area alone at night, or someone around us might be sick and contagious. Our brain sends our body signals to be alert, be aware, be prepared—to be anxious!

Anxiety can be mental (giving us messages to believe), emotional (triggering feelings), and physiological (causing changes in our body). It's not always bad. Anxiety is a good gift from God intended for our safety. We need it! But what if we feel anxious when there is no real threat? What if the threat is gone and we're still anxious? That's when anxiety is bad.

Our anxiety is wrongly awakened all the time! We live in a culture that is more than happy to trigger our anxiety. Our twenty-four-hour news cycles, quick-fix approaches to life and faith, and a host of self-soothing alternatives keep us disconnected from the life of trust, peace, and healthy risk taking that God intends for us.

You're reading this book because you or someone you love is struggling with anxiety. Maybe you feel restless, worried, or preoccupied with concerns most days. You battle unrealistic expectations of yourself. You fear being embarrassed, criticized, or judged by others. You're uncomfortable in everyday interactions with other people. You are not as assertive as you want to be. Or worse.

Maybe you have intrusive thoughts, unwanted feelings, and intense fear about specific situations or objects. You've had some terrible experiences in your past and are now flooded with thoughts and feelings you don't understand. Maybe you've learned to address your fears by engaging in certain rituals that make you feel less anxious, but now you're dependent on those rituals. Or you might be experiencing panic attacks, sudden and overwhelming feelings of anxiety that have interfered with your life.

Does any of this sound familiar? If so, you are not alone.

We all have anxiety, but we can learn to live rich and meaningful lives without being controlled by it. That's what this book is all about.

How to Read this Book

When I went through personal counseling, I took copious notes. I read articles, listened to podcasts, spoke with other professionals, and read great books on the subject. As I found things that resonated with me, I made notes in my phone so they were always with me. This became like my own personal field guide. This book is made up of what was most helpful to me on my own path to healthier habits. Here's how I recommend you use this book.

Read one section at a time, in order. This book is divided into thirty short sections, designed for you to read one section per day to help you learn and practice skills you'll need. Try to resist the urge to read more than one section at a time or skip ahead, because each section builds on the next. The goal is not to fly through it in thirty days but to develop healthy habits, so . . .

Practice what you are learning. Each section has action steps. These are important. Unlike some forms of counseling, freedom from anxiety is based in what's called a *cognitive-behavioral approach*. This simply means that our thinking should lead to changes in behavior. We learn by doing. I provide different kinds of action steps to try.

Take your time and go back if you need to. The book has thirty sections, but don't feel like you have to get through this book in thirty days. If you feel like you need to stay in a section for a while or revisit a section that resonated with you, do it! You might even feel anxiety while reading. That may be because you are bumping up against some important growth points. Don't give up.

Also, you'll notice that the book is designed to integrate anxiety treatment principles and the Bible. If you've had negative or painful experiences with God, religion, or faith, hang in there with me. I've been there too. Whether you are already a follower of Jesus, are coming back to God after a time of being away, or are just looking into faith, my hope is that you'll experience this book as an invitation to a new life with God.

Four Principles You Need to Know

As we start *The Anxiety Field Guide*, we're heading on a well-trodden path. There are many great resources on anxiety, and they are all rooted in four principles.

- Normalization: Accept that anxiety is natural but can become unhealthy.

- Exposure: Understand your fears and begin facing them rather than avoiding them.

- Habituation: Use new skills to become desensitized to your fears.

- Care: Discover healthy ways to experience God's love for you and others.

I've chosen to visit and revisit these principles throughout the book in different ways rather than group readings under each principle. This way, if you choose to read a section daily, you'll be invited to explore and apply each principle every week.

My understanding of these principles has been profoundly shaped by four thought leaders: Scott Symington, Jeffrey Schwartz, David Burns, and Max Lucado. Do yourself a favor and familiarize yourself with their work. They provide the foundation for what you'll be reading throughout this book. But I don't intend them or this book as a replacement for professional help, especially if you are feeling hopeless, suicidal, or experiencing self-harm. Find a professional who can help you find the support you need.

Let's Head to the Waterfall

In 2012, my family and I spent two weeks in Costa Rica. We stayed at a retreat house for pastors and missionaries. During one of our first days there, our host took my sons and me across the street to the entrance of a gorgeous rainforest. A sign there simply read WATERFALL, with an arrow pointing into the forest.

"Let's go!" our host said.

"That's it? No map?" I asked.

As he started to lead the way, he said, "There's a path, but sometimes it changes. We'll just follow the sound of the water, and we'll get there." So off we went! The path was there, but sometimes we had to stop, rethink things, and circle back a bit. But we finally got there, and it was worth all the work. The cold mountain water created a cool mist that pierced the humid air.

The next day, I asked my wife to go to the waterfall with me. She also asked, "No map?" I gave the answer I had been given: "There's a path, but sometimes it changes. We'll just follow the sound of the water, and we'll get there."

Off we went, two naive Southern Californians, into a Costa Rican rainforest in search of a waterfall. The path was less clear, and I forgot things, made mistakes, and had to stop and gather my thoughts. Sometimes we circled back. My wife was an encouraging companion.

We finally made it! It was worth all the work . . . again!

Navigating anxiety is a lot like going to that waterfall. Others have blazed a path, but it's also yours to find for yourself. It might be a little different for you than it was for them. You'll make mistakes, circle back, and try new things.

And when the path is unclear, I want to encourage you to keep listening. That waterfall is the gentle and powerful sound of God's love inviting you to come experience what Jesus called "a rich and satisfying life" (John 10:10). And remember, God's love is not a one-time trip to the waterfall. It's an invitation to come back again and again, maybe even bringing someone else with you next time.

Let's head to the waterfall!

1

Relax, It's Just Your Brain

Your brain is designed to warn you of danger,
but sometimes it sends you false alarms.
You can be thankful for your brain while
retraining it to respond differently.

I **WAS ALONE IN MY OFFICE** at work when I heard a fire alarm. It startled me. "Is there a fire?" I thought. "Where is it coming from? Do I need to leave?" I gathered a few things and hustled down the hallway only to find some of my coworkers huddled in our small break room. One of them told me, "Someone was toasting some bread and the crumbs in the toaster triggered the fire alarm." We laughed it off and went back to work.

It happened a couple more times over the next few weeks. The alarm would sound, I'd get startled and pop my head out the door, someone would point to the toaster, and we'd roll our eyes. After three or four more times I wondered why we didn't clean or replace the toaster. I got used to telling myself, "If it's a real fire, someone will come get me."

One day, I was meeting with a member of our church in my office and the alarm went off again. She was startled and also confused as to why I wasn't even reacting to the sound. She finally asked, "Umm . . . is there a fire?" Without thinking, I replied, "Oh, no. It's not a fire, it's a bagel."

I remember this so vividly because it happened right around the time that I was learning about how our brains help us (and don't help us) when it comes to fear and anxiety. What I learned was probably the single most important insight on the path of freedom from my chronic worry, intrusive thoughts, and unwanted feelings: our brains are wonderfully designed to help us respond to threats, but sometimes our brains are wrong.

Imagine if I were hiding behind a door and shouted "boo!" as you entered. Before you could think about what was happening, your brain would dilate your eyes so you could see better, signal your renal glands to produce adrenaline for more energy, and trigger your heart to direct more blood to your extremities. This is done to ready you for four potential responses: fight (resist), flight (avoid), freeze (lock up), or fawn (people please). This all comes from a little almond-shaped area of your brain called the *amygdala*. It's the threat center of your brain, and in that moment, it shouts, "Be afraid!"

Then you realize it's just me shouting "boo!" The thinking area of your brain takes over. You breathe deeply, your heart rate slows, eyes adjust, and nervous energy subsides. You laugh a little (or punch me) because you realize there is no reason to be afraid.

Here's the good news: Without even thinking, the threat center in your brain quickly assessed the possible dangers and jumped into action to prepare you for how to deal with the problem. When the threat was over, your brain reassessed the situation. Your fear and anxiety changed to other emotions and responses.

Here's the bad news: Sometimes our brains don't readjust. Sometimes the threat or perceived threat is gone, but our hearts are still pumping out of our chests, our minds are still racing, and we are still filled with energy. While this is happening in our brain and body, we become restless:

- We have a sense that we are in danger when we aren't.

- We feel like we did something wrong and don't know how to make it right.

- We're sure we forgot to do something but can't figure out what it was.

- We overthink our appearance, health, safety, reputation, and self-worth.

- We decide that the most important thing to do is get rid of these bad feelings.

- We panic, thinking we've lost touch with God, others, or ourselves.

This is anxiety—and it starts in our brain.

Just like that fire alarm at work, your brain is doing its job. Your brain is trying to warn you of danger and get you ready for action. Most of the time this is happening without you knowing it. Thank God!

Sometimes your threat center lights up when there's no threat at all, or it lights up and won't turn off. This is called *amygdala hijacking*. It's when your feeling-self overrides your thinking-self, sending you well-intentioned false alarms.

Why does this happen? We're not exactly sure.

It could be chemical. Emotions are biochemical reactions in the brain that we perceive as expressions of who we are and what we think. What we experience as fear is a cocktail of chemicals being released from the amygdala to the rest of our brain and body.

It could be conditioning. Our brains are always collecting data for future use. If we've always feared something, our brains will help us continue to be scared. If we've learned to be afraid, we might have to start unlearning it.

Anxiety and fear are intended for our good, but for whatever reason they can also cause problems.

When people say, "Don't worry!" they're trying to talk us out of our anxiety. But it's not that simple. Well-meaning advice or quick fixes are rarely helpful for those of us with anxiety. In fact, they often make us feel guilty or embarrassed. We don't want to be anxious. Managing our anxiety can end up feeling like a full-time job.

But there's hope! Let's start this journey with what is called *normalization*—learning to accept that anxiety is natural.

ACTION STEPS

1. *Take a moment to be grateful.* The next time you feel anxious or afraid, find a place to sit down. Breathe deeply, feel your feet on the ground, and be aware of your body and your surroundings. Read Psalm 139:13-14, which says, "You made all the delicate, inner parts of my body / and knit me together in my mother's womb. / Thank you for making me so wonderfully complex!" These simple exercises can help you slow down and quietly be thankful for being present in the moment.

2. *Blame your brain.* One of the most liberating truths that I've learned has been to pass off some responsibility to my brain and not carry it all myself. You have an oversensitive amygdala. Put the responsibility where it belongs. You're starting to take responsibility for your own wellness. Begin by accepting that some of what's happening in you is neurological and chemical, and it's happening outside of your control and choosing.

3. *Give yourself permission to not fix what you are feeling.* It is very common to be anxious about our anxiety. Trying to stop your brain from doing what it's done for years can lead to frustration, self-condemnation, and exhaustion. This will take a little time. In your next anxious moments, speak some encouraging words to yourself. Remind yourself that you are just getting started, and this will get better as you keep at it.

2

Be Open to Uncertainty

Anxiety is a form of dis-ease.
It's having difficulty with the unknown.
Finding peace of mind involves learning
to tolerate more uncertainty.

M Y FRIEND JONATHAN has celiac disease. It's a disorder of the digestive system that causes the immune system to attack his small intestine when gluten is present. Gluten is a protein found in foods that contain wheat, barley, or rye. He has to be careful because his intolerance to gluten can flare up and cause digestive trouble, fatigue, irritability, depression, and a variety of other serious health problems.

He's super active, healthy, and positive because he's learned a lot about celiac disease and about himself. He enjoys a great diet because he's learned how to manage what he takes in so he can stay healthy. I can't relate to Jonathan's intolerance to gluten because I love gluten! More gluten, please. But I can relate to Jonathan because I have an intolerance as well.

I have an intolerance to uncertainty.

Anxiety is a natural response to facing the unknown. Everyone faces unknowns and uncertainties. We ask, What will happen with my health, family, job, finances, friendships, weather, or schedule?

Some people enjoy facing uncertainty. They love change. They are quickly bored with routines. Their motto is "If it ain't broke, break it!" What we call anxiety, they call excitement! The unknown is a great adventure for them. I can't relate.

I like predictability. I am risk averse. I want to know what's coming up so I can prepare for it. The more uncertainty there is, the sicker I get. When my intolerance to uncertainty flares up, I get the four I's: irregularity, irritability, insomnia, and irrationalism.

Like Jonathan, I need to be aware of what I am taking in (watching, reading, listening). But unlike Jonathan with his disease, the way forward with my dis-ease is not by avoiding uncertainty but being open to it.

Anxiety is about control. It's about wanting to understand and prepare for life's uncertainties. There's nothing wrong with wanting to be prepared. That's just responsible. But life is filled with so much uncertainty that it's impossible to be prepared for everything.

Those of us who struggle with anxiety don't get anxious about everything. Maybe that's what makes anxiety so confusing. People with anxiety are often thoughtful, productive, and compassionate people. We take risks all the time and step into all kinds of new situations with no problems at all—but there are some areas that cause our anxiety to go through the roof! I've gone skydiving and driven a NASCAR, and I speak in front of thousands of people every week. No problem! But I get very anxious at social events and when making big decisions that could negatively impact people.

What brings you anxiety?

Anxiety happens when we feel out of control in a way that is unique to us. We feel insecure and will do anything to get rid of that feeling. In a way, our anxiety isn't just an intolerance to uncertainty but an addiction to certainty. The addiction is aggravated by our culture, which idolizes certainty and control. We want mysteries to be solved, problems to be fixed, and doubts to be resolved.

When I first started to realize my own struggle with anxiety, I went to some trusted leaders at my church. I wanted them to pray for me. I said, "I struggle with anxiety. I struggle with uncertainty and the unknown. I have all these questions in my brain, like, Am I a good person? Am I doing my job right? Are people upset with me? Am I prepared for the future? And every time I look for certainty and assurance, it's never enough. So I think I need prayer that I could learn to live with uncertainty."

They were so gracious. They stood up in a circle around me, lovingly placed their hands on my shoulders, and took turns praying, "God, help Jason to know beyond a shadow of a doubt that you are with him. Help him to know for certain that he's a good man and that's he's doing a great job. Let that be as clear to him as it is to us. Thank you for giving him that certainty. Amen!"

When they finished, I asked them to sit down for a moment. I said, "I love you. Thank you so much for that prayer, but I'm not sure if you understand what I'm saying. That prayer was exactly opposite of what I need. I don't need clarity; I'm addicted to assurance. And my relapsing is going from person to person, prayer to prayer, book to book, behavior to behavior, trying to eliminate this anxious feeling of uncertainty. I need to be open to uncertainty."

They thanked me for clarifying and then asked if they could try again. Then they prayed, "God, you love us whether we believe it or feel it. Thank you. Give Jason certainty where he can have it, and when it's not there, help him to continue to trust you and keep doing what he needs to do. And surround him with people to listen and love when he's having a tough time. Amen."

That prayer was awesome because it balanced the knowable and unknowable. It reminded me of one of my favorite quotes from the Bible, which says, "The secret things belong to the LORD our God, but the things revealed belong to us and to our children" (Deuteronomy 29:29 NIV). Some things in life will always be shrouded in mystery, but there is a loving God who will let us know what we need to know.

As we continue this journey, let's take a break from the hours we've spent manically skimming books and internet articles looking for information, lengthy phone calls with people to get reassurance, and sleepless nights trying to answer the unknowns. Let's try to embrace the idea that uncertainty is not bad, it's normal. It's a part of life—part of the mystery of what it means to be human. It might feel counter-intuitive, but it's the way forward.

ACTION STEPS

1. *Create a certainty list.* Make a list of values, beliefs, and con-victions of which you are certain. For example, you may not be certain that you are 100 percent healthy, but you might be sure that you are healthy enough to read this book and engage in relationships with the people who care about you. Include ob-jective truths as well as your values, beliefs, relationships, and skills. When you find yourself focused on what you don't know, revisit this list to ground yourself in what you know for sure.

2. *Make more room for uncertainty.* Identify one area of uncertainty to work on. What is one situation, relationship, or issue that does not appear to have a clear resolution? There are probably many, but choose one to experiment with. Maybe you could decide to leave it unresolved until you finish reading this book. Instead of trying to find certainty, try saying, "I don't know yet." This phrase may feel like an expression of failure. Consider reframing the phrase "I don't know" as a statement of accepting reality. Again, the goal is not to eliminate uncertainty but to learn to live with it.

3. *Give your uncertainties to God.* When you're feeling anxious about uncertainty, spend a quiet moment with God. It could be in the form of a prayer, taking a deep breath, or simply remem-bering that God is with you. In those moments, try to embrace uncertainty as part of the much larger story of your life that God is lovingly writing.

3

Observe Before You Own

When you have intrusive thoughts
and unwanted feelings, you can develop
a practice of experiencing these thoughts
and feelings without endorsing them.

O NE DAY MY WIFE, Marie, called to me in a panic. "Jason, I just got this alert that there's a serious problem with my software, and the company is requesting access to my laptop so they can help me out! I think I have a virus!"

As we read what was popping up on the screen, we discovered a couple of things. First, we didn't have the software the alert was warning us about. Second, there were spelling errors in the message. We took some time to observe what the warning said and then . . . we ignored it.

That alert was what's called *fear-ware*. Fear-ware is any ad, pop-up, or solicitation designed to suck people in by getting them scared. It operates on the assumption that people will believe the information their computer is giving them. It almost worked on us.

What was true with a computer is true of our brains. We can't believe everything we think. We all experience thoughts and feelings that don't represent who we are, what we believe, or what we desire.

Maybe you've believed one of these three myths about your thoughts and feelings:

Myth 1: I can control all my thoughts. We can control some of our thoughts, but sometimes thoughts just "pop up." These are called *automatic thoughts*. Everyone has them. Ideas and information pop into our heads all the time without our choosing.

It reminds me of a scene in the movie *Ghostbusters*. An evil, invisible entity wants to destroy New York and says it will embody whatever form the Ghostbusters are thinking of at that moment. They quickly agree to clear their minds of any thoughts, but within seconds the evil entity begins to destroy New York in the form of one of their childhood memories: the Stay-Puft Marshmallow Man. They look around wondering who had that thought in their mind. The guilty Ghostbuster confesses, "I couldn't help it. It just popped in there!"

Myth 2: My automatic thoughts represent the true me. Many of us fall into the trap of believing that all our thoughts and feelings bubble up from some core truth about ourselves or fundamental aspect of our character. But most automatic thoughts and feelings carry no meaning at all.

I was in Las Vegas recently. I was overlooking the Las Vegas Strip from a balcony and suddenly imagined myself jumping. Have you ever had this thought? It's not uncommon for people standing in a high place. Most people who have a thought like this are not suicidal—so why does it happen? We're not sure. But automatic thoughts of hurting yourself or someone else doesn't mean this is what you really want to do, are meant to do, or should do.

Myth 3: If I feel it, it must be true. Our culture perpetuates this belief. And what make this myth convincing is that we often make decisions based on our feelings. But just because you feel something doesn't mean it's true.

I was feeling guilty the other day. I called my friend and asked, "Did I offend you when we talked on the phone a few days ago? I've been feeling like I did."

He said, "No!"

We talked about it more and he added, "I wish you could have called me when that feeling came up. I could have saved you from a couple days of worrying about it." We need to investigate our feelings to decide how we should respond to them.

These three myths about our thoughts and feelings can send us into spirals of worry, doubt, and confusion because we mistake our automatic thoughts and feelings with our core values, beliefs, and convictions. So an important healthy habit for long-lasting healing is observing our thoughts and feelings before owning them.

I have an app on my phone called Headspace. The creators of Headspace suggest that we imagine ourselves sitting on the side of the road and watching cars go back and forth. Big cars and little cars, fast and slow, different sizes and colors, going the same way and opposite ways. These cars represent our thoughts and feelings. There is a lot going on, and our first impulse might be to jump into that street and start directing traffic. But they suggest imagining yourself just sitting and observing the traffic.

The idea is simple. When a thought or feeling pops into your mind, instead of believing it, correcting it, or trying to shut it down, just identify it nonjudgmentally. When we accept that unwanted thoughts and feelings happen, we can calmly acknowledge our anxiety as something we have and are working on. It's another part of normalization and will prepare us for our next steps to lasting healing.

I applied this a few weeks ago in my life. I sat down to write this section of the book and was suddenly flooded with unwanted thoughts and feelings. My leg started bouncing, I couldn't focus, and this thought popped into my mind: *This book isn't going to help anyone!* My first thought was to try to extinguish the thought. Instead, I decided to take a moment and observe it. I thought, *How interesting that my leg is bouncing and my mind is racing*, and instead of believing the self-defeating message in my mind, I said, *Wow, that's a really critical thought that popped into my head.*

Do you see the difference? In the most nonjudgmental way possible, I just made observations about my thoughts and feelings rather than owning them. Now, you might be asking, "But what if the thought is wrong? I need to correct it, change it, fix it . . . right?" Absolutely, that's part of the larger process of what's called *cognitive restructuring.* That's when we begin changing how to process our thoughts and feelings to align more with our core beliefs and reality. We'll talk about that later.

This is a good point to remind ourselves of the importance of self-acceptance. Brennan Manning once said, "Genuine self-acceptance is not derived from the power of positive thinking, mind games or pop psychology. It is an act of faith in the God of grace" (Brennan Manning, *The Ragamuffin Gospel*). A lot of our anxiety comes from our well-intentioned desire to be a good person and make good decisions. Those of us with anxiety have a high sense of responsibility. Self-acceptance is a way of giving the full weight of responsibility to God and learning to rest in Jesus.

ACTION STEPS

1. *Label your automatic thoughts and feelings.* Next time you have a thought or feeling that just pops into your head, stop and label it as an "automatic thought or feeling." Tell yourself that you did not choose to have that thought or feeling, so God does not require you to immediately believe it or obey it. Remind yourself that it doesn't necessarily reflect who you are, what you believe, or what is true.

2. *Use nonjudgmental vocabulary.* When you have an automatic thought or feeling, don't judge yourself for having it. If it's a critical message—something like, *You're ugly*—consider playfully greeting it like, *Oh, hello, unsolicited thought!* If

you have a physical expression of anxiety, try referring to your body's sensations. For example, instead of saying, "I am so scared. I'm such a coward," try saying, "My heart is racing, and my palms are sweaty."

3. ***Identify the myths you believe about thoughts and feelings.*** Reread the three myths in this section. Which one most strongly resonates with you? Is this a myth you were "taught" at some point or was it something you "caught" while growing up?

4

Practice Pit Stops

In each experience of anxiety, there is a moment
of awareness in which you can decide
what to tell yourself and how you will respond.
Make the most of those moments.

A **FRIEND OF MINE** who works for NASCAR once invited me to watch one of the races from his executive suite. Someone once said, "NASCAR is great if you're a fan of left turns." Being there myself, I can say it's about more than left turns! It was exhilarating, and I spent the time asking my friend a lot of questions. Here's what I learned.

When a driver is hitting those turns and straightaways at over a hundred miles per hour, two things are happening—the tires are wearing down and the gas is running out. That's expected. But the driver can't finish the race on worn tires and an empty tank. There is a moment of decision in which the driver has to ask, "Do I need to come in for the pit stop or do I keep going?" It can make or break winning the race.

About halfway through the race my friend asked, "Do you want to go down into the pits?" I was like, "Um . . . yeah!" Have you ever watched the cars come in for a pit stop? It's an amazing thing to watch. Tires are changed, the car is refueled, adjustments are made, and then the driver is given a "go" signal, and they are back in the race.

It all happens in ten seconds.

Ten seconds can change the entire outcome of the day.

We tend to think that the answers to our biggest problems require hours, maybe even years, of deep introspective therapy or medication, but researchers have found that, just like in a NASCAR race, ten seconds can make a huge difference in changing our learned patterns of thinking and feeling.

I want you to imagine your struggles with anxiety as the growling engine of that car. When you face a moment of chronic worry, an intrusive thought, or an unwanted feeling, imagine that you are running low on gas and your tires are wearing down. You might want to put the pedal to the floor to get out of it or just slam on the brakes because you feel something is wrong. Instead, try pulling into a pit stop. Ten seconds may be all you need.

Here's what practicing pit stops looks like in my life.

Recognize my need for help. This is when I say to myself, "I'm having an anxious moment." Sometimes this is easy to recognize, like having a panic attack. Other times it is more subtle, like a heavy sigh that someone else notices before I do. This first step has been the hardest for me because my previous way of dealing with anxiety was to ignore it, push through it, or try to extinguish it. Recognizing a need for a pit stop is the first step.

Pause what I am doing. In my most anxious moments, it's like I'm on autopilot. My heart is racing, my leg is bouncing, and my thoughts are going everywhere (or nowhere). To reboot my brain, I'll change my posture, take a deep breath, stretch my neck, smell a calming aroma, focus on a different task, or quietly pray. Like a NASCAR driver, these are ways to take back the wheel from my "feeling self" in a nonaggressive way and continue my race as planned.

Allow myself ten seconds. The biggest excuse for not taking care of myself is "I don't have the time." I am a driven, responsible, and others-focused person. I worry that self-care will take away from more important things. But for a NASCAR driver, ten seconds is a strategic and calculated use of time. And that's all the time I need when I am in my anxious moments!

Call anxiety what it is. This is when I try to just label anxiety for what it is: an out-of-control feeling generated by my brain that may not represent reality. I also try to identify what's going on in my mind, body, and heart. Am I feeling confused, angry, lonely, sad, restless? I might not know what is going on. That's okay too. I'm not trying to fix, change, or extinguish my anxiety. I'm just taking ten seconds to label it.

Use a field guide skill. In this last step, I choose something from all my learned skills and decide which one best applies to my unique situation. Just like a NASCAR driver might have a different need at each pit stop, not every anxious moment has the same solution. Do I need to say a simple or vulnerable prayer, confront a core belief, reach out to a loved one, enjoy a healthy habit, stay in the feeling and expose it more, put it in the worry box, drink some water, or just make a decision? This is where this book will come in handy!

You're probably thinking, *All this can happen in ten seconds?* Yes. It only takes a few seconds for anxiety to flood us with chaos. We only need seconds to begin the process of regaining control. But the most important step is recognizing the need for a pit stop. It's a moment of choice or "agency." It's a moment of awareness where you can begin to regain control.

As you begin this practice, you might only realize this moment after the fact. You'll say, "Shoot, I had a moment of clarity when I could have just stopped and gathered myself. I missed it." If that happens, don't beat yourself up. You spotted it! When you get there again, try to take it. When that happens to me, I imagine myself as a NASCAR driver who missed the pit stop entry. I tell myself, "I'll do one more lap and then go in."

ACTION STEPS

1. *When anxious, give yourself ten seconds.* The next time you feel anxious, give yourself permission to take a conscious ten seconds for yourself. Take a deep breath and tell yourself you are having an anxious moment. Gently and slowly count to ten. Like the action step in the first reading, consider taking a moment of gratitude for being present in the moment.

2. *Give yourself more than ten seconds if needed.* If you can, write down a few thoughts, feelings, and observations about what is happening with your body. I keep a notes page on my phone just for this purpose. If I am with others and need a few minutes, I will excuse myself to go to the bathroom and use that time to take notes and "reboot my brain." The goal is to give yourself some brief moments to regather yourself so you can reengage with your life.

   Create a mood log. Track your anxious moments, intrusive thoughts, and unwanted feelings to help you find any patterns to your anxiety. Do you notice that you experience more anxiety at certain times, in specific situations, or with particular people? Creating a mood log can help you prepare for better decision making in the future. I'm including one of my own mood logs here as an example. But there are great mood logs online that you can download as well as programs for mobile tracking of your mood.

Table 4.1. Mood log

MOOD LOG	INCIDENT	THOUGHT	FEELING	INTENSITY	NOTES
SUNDAY	morning church services	I am excited!	encouraged, joy	8	
	evening church services	I could have done better. Did I help anyone?	depressed, restless	6	These are emotionally difficult car drives home. How can I better prepare for this drive?
	evening workout	I need some time by myself.	peaceful, cathartic	8	
MONDAY	study time	This is important time for God, others, and me.	energized, curious, thankful	7	I need to make sure I do this in the mornings, not afternoons.
	returning emails	I'd better do this now.	accomplished, relieved	6	Glad I did that.
	conversation with critic	People don't understand me.	angry, confused	7	These are draining to me. When and how can I do them differently?
	afternoon meetings	I don't want to be here.	exhausted, withdrawn	4	
	evening workout	I'm not in the mood but my future self will thank me.	determined, withdrawn	4	Remember that you will not always be in the mood to do what's good for you.
TUESDAY	staff meeting	I am honored to work with these people.	grateful, happy	8	
	lunch with colleague	Not sure what this lunch is for.	pensive, thoughtful	6	Not what I thought it would be.
	hospital visits	I miss doing this.	purposeful, fulfilled	9	I need to find more time for this.
	evening teaching @ school	This is fun, but I wouldn't want this as a job.	energized, joyful	9	
WEDNESDAY	morning meetings	I don't know what I am doing.	restless, anxious	7	I need to do meetings in the afternoon instead.

	HR discussion	Making sure people are treated fairly is important to me.	responsible	6	How could I improve on this? Am I making room to celebrate how important this is to me?
	family get-together	I want time alone!	stressed, detached	4	
	evening workout	I have so much to do.	stressed	6	
THURSDAY	leadership retreat	Am I a good leader?	curious, contented	8	
	community meeting	What great people!	happy	8	I'd like to do this more.
	budgeting meeting	Ugh!	frustrated, anxious	4	I'd like to do this less.
	evening work on taxes	I'm so disorganized.	frustrated, scared	10	I am organized and prepared, but this is a trigger.
FRIDAY	going to estate sales	Me time!!	relaxed, curious	10	
	downtime with family	I like this, but should I be doing something?	relaxed, restless	9	Learn to live with the tension of doing nothing.
	evening workout	I'm glad I'm taking care of myself.	empowered, motivated	8	
SATURDAY	home projects	I wish I had more help with this.	determined, frustrated	6	
	date with Marie	Can I just retire and spend it all like this?	happy, peaceful	10	I wish we'd have planned some more in advance.
	evening sermon rehearsal	I am nervous but in a fun way.	excited, hopeful	9	I have some underlying fear that this message will fall flat.

5

You Are Not Alone

Anxiety grows in solitude.
Rather than isolating in embarrassment,
you can invite God and trusted loved ones
into your anxiety.

W HEN MY DAUGHTER WAS YOUNG, she had her own room. She loved it—except at bedtime. She was afraid of going to bed alone. So I would read her a book, pray, and then lie down in bed with her for a few minutes until she went to sleep. This was really comforting to her. When I look back on those years, I'm so glad I had that time with her.

One of those nights stands out in my memory. We read, prayed, and turned off the lights. It was dark and quiet. We had been lying there for about ten minutes when my daughter quietly asked, "Dad, are you still here?" I said yes, and she was soon off to sleep. I asked her about this a few nights later. She said, "Sometimes I'm still awake, but I'm not sure if you are gone yet. I spend a couple of minutes wondering if I should ask if you are still there." My heart just broke imagining her in those couple of minutes, wondering if she's alone.

Anxiety is lonely. In our most anxious moments of panic, restless thinking, fear, and ruminating, it feels like no one can help us. Like my daughter in that dark and quiet moment, our anxious hearts ask,

"Is anyone there? Does anyone understand what I am going through? Am I alone?"

You are not alone.

It might feel like you are alone. But you aren't.

Anxiety can be embarrassing. That's a very normal feeling. We may feel like nobody understands our struggle, so we hide. We isolate. It feels safer. In our insecurity about the unknown, we move to a place of control. Since we can't control the responses of others, we tend to shut them out and go it alone.

Our negative experiences may have also taught us to hide. The first time I talked about my anxiety at church, a well-intentioned woman told me she believed that I had a "spirit of fear" and asked if she could pray over me to "remove that evil spirit permanently." This only made me go back into hiding again. I have to continue to remind myself that I don't have to isolate.

Personality also plays into our anxiety. I'm an introvert. I'm a thinker and a dreamer. I spend a lot of time exploring ideas in my head. This allows me to be strategic, creative, and empathetic. I believe this is part of how God made me. It also has a shadow side. I ruminate on things, and left unchecked, my overthinking can drive me to greater anxiety. I have to be careful about ruminating alone.

Some of us have managed our anxiety through relationships in not-so-healthy ways. We may know someone with a problem they cannot solve. We feel like if we can't help them, we have less value. We can become obsessed with helping. This can be rooted in something called *anxious attachment.* Anxious attachment happens when our early relationships did not provide the assurance and protection we needed. As we grow older, we may feel incomplete without a partner, be drawn to toxic relationships, or become compulsive in trying to help people. In these situations, our relationships may reinforce our anxiety rather than help us find freedom.

Healthy relationships are so important in long-lasting healing from anxiety. They are one way we care for ourselves. They can encourage us, comfort us, and challenge us. Relationships with God and others are where we can feel accepted and known. They also help us to keep moving forward.

Here are some characteristics of healthy relationships.

Vulnerability. Anxiety causes us to want to protect ourselves, so we need relationships where we can be honest with each other. But relationships are messy. They are fragile and involve risk. Rather than hiding what we're thinking or feeling, we can tell people what's going on inside of us. Instead of protecting ourselves from harm, we can tell people that we have felt harmed. We can let them know what triggers us and how they can help us in our anxious moments. We can also admit our anxious "push/pull" behaviors. We push people away ("You hurt me!") and then pull them closer ("Do you care about me?"). As we work on getting healthier, we can confess how confusing this is to those who are closest to us.

Mutuality. Anxiety usually shows itself in imbalanced relationships. We are either the helpers or in constant need of others' help. But we need relationships where we care for each other equally. If we are helpers in the relationship, we can try expressing our needs and wants to the other person and let them help us. It may feel selfish, but it's not. We can also learn that listening is a form of helping. If we are continually seeking reassurance and comfort from the other person (or people), we can try letting unsolicited comfort and reassurance come naturally in the relationship. It's okay to ask for reassurance, but having questions, doubts, and some anxiety is normal in close relationships.

Playfulness. Anxiety causes us to see the world as a serious place. We may feel that every conversation must be deep and every interaction "productive." We need relationships where we can laugh together, have fun together, and enjoy each other's company without having to solve a problem, analyze our feelings, or come to each other's rescue. Joy and laughter release tension and stress. I try to keep them as a priority.

The most important relationship in life is our relationship with God. Whether we feel or believe it, God is with us all the time. That is God's repeated promise throughout Scripture (Psalm 23:4; Isaiah 41:10; Matthew 28:20; Romans 8:38-39). When we feel the most alone, misunderstood, and confused, the little child in us asks, "Is anyone there? Am I alone?"

God says, "I am with you."

Appreciating God's presence, rather than trying to make God proud, has been something I've been trying to grow more to understand. In the past, I would come to God with all my successes and accomplishments. I wanted a cosmic pat on the back. Other times, I'd come to God with a list of problems hoping for a supernatural fix that would take away my problems and my anxious feelings. But I'm learning that in my most anxious times, I can come to God and experience something much more helpful—God's presence, acceptance, and love.

ACTION STEPS

1. *Identify your most life-giving relationships.* Make a short list of the people with whom you feel loved, accepted, and known. Who do you feel safest to express your thoughts and feelings with? Who do you feel less alone with? Who in your life has expressed similar struggles with anxiety? Take time this week to thank them for their presence in your life.

2. *Grow in your close relationships.* Reread the three characteristics of healthy relationships: vulnerability, mutuality, and playfulness. Are you experiencing these with the people you included on your short list? How could you experiment with more vulnerability, mutuality, or playfulness? Perhaps you could ask someone closest to you to read this book as well and discuss how it could affect your relationship.

3. *Reflect on God's promised presence in your life.* In your next anxious moment, rather than asking God to take away your

anxiety or fix the problem, try to remember that God is with you in that moment. Don't try to feel God's presence. Read God's promises (Psalm 23:4; Isaiah 41:10; Matthew 28:20; Romans 8:38-39) and accept them as true, even if your feelings don't align with them. Thank God for being present and not judging you for feeling the way you do.

6

Pray Like Jesus

Anxiety can turn prayer into a restless attempt
to find predictability and reassurance.
Jesus invites you to pray with simplicity
and vulnerability.

I **HAVE A HEAVY-DUTY TOOL BAG** in my garage that holds all my
tools. I've been meaning to get a peg board and hang all my tools
above my workbench so I can easily find them. For now, they are
still in the bag. The other day I needed to repair something in the
house. I went out to the garage and started digging around in
the bag.

It was frustrating. There were a lot of tools in there and I couldn't
find the right one. I grabbed the tool at the top of the bag and said, "I
guess I could use this for the job." Almost immediately I remembered
this conventional wisdom: use the wrong tool for the job, and you
mess up the job . . . and the tool.

Digging through that tool bag for the right tool made me think
about how I've struggled with prayer in my life. Prayer is sometimes like me searching for the right words, language, techniques,
and forms of prayer to try getting God to answer me and give me
what I need.

I remember praying one night, "God, my mind is going a mile a minute. I can't sleep. I'm so worried. Give me peace. Give me an answer to this problem. Help me think about this thing in just the right way so I can rest my mind." I was digging and searching for the right tool, but I couldn't find it. Maybe you can relate.

Maybe you pray in a restless way.

Maybe your anxiety has caused you to give up on prayer.

Maybe you don't pray—but you wonder if it could help.

When Jesus taught people about prayer, he tried to address that same restless searching that I experience (and maybe you do too). People in Jesus' day believed that if they said long prayers, repeated the same prayers, or had some kind of supernatural prayer language, God would be more likely to hear them and give them what they needed. This created a lot of anxiety for people.

Wherever you are in your relationship between anxiety and prayer, I believe Jesus has two words that can help you in your relationship with God in prayer: *simplicity* and *vulnerability*.

Let's look at the first word: *simplicity*.

Jesus' approach to prayer was dramatically simple. While others in his day were digging around in their religious tool bags, borrowing every kind of approach and technique to figure out how to relate to God, Jesus suggested a stripped-down template commonly known as the Lord's Prayer. While many people have prayed this prayer word for word, it's not only a prescription but also a description of things God recommends get our focus. This prayer has been written and prayed in a lot of different forms. Here are the basics:

> Our Father in heaven, hallowed be your name, your kingdom come,
>> your will be done, on earth as it is in heaven.
>> Give us today our daily bread.
>> And forgive us our sins, as we also forgive those who sin against us.

And lead us not into temptation but deliver us from the evil one.

For yours is the kingdom and the power and the glory forever.

Amen. (see Matthew 6:9-13; Luke 11:2-4)

When we're anxious, prayer can turn into all-night wrestling matches for answers, blessings, and wisdom. When we are obsessing, prayer can become a compulsive ritual like handwashing, ruminating, or hoarding. It looks noble because it's a spiritual act, but we may just be trying to extinguish our anxious thoughts and feelings.

Prayer is a way to remind ourselves that we are always in the presence of God. Prayer also reminds us that God loves us and has plans that are greater than we can imagine. We are reminded to "give all your worries and cares to God, for he cares about you" (1 Peter 5:7). We can find great peace and comfort from prayer, but it is not a magic formula for eliminating anxiety.

I used to go on and on in my prayers, hoping that if I prayed long enough or eloquently enough, my anxiety would be relieved. But that has changed. Now, when I am anxious, sometimes I'll pray the Lord's Prayer (verbatim or in my own words) and then be done. My temptation is to keep going because it doesn't feel done. I am learning to have meaningful, brief encounters with God in prayer rather than using prayer as a tool for God to get rid of my anxiety.

Let's look at the second word: *vulnerability*.

How did Jesus pray when he was anxious? Thankfully, the writers of Jesus' life story made sure to include two dramatic moments of prayer from Jesus' life when he was full of anxiety. These can help us pray when we are anxious.

One of these anxious moments was the night Jesus was arrested. He knew he would be killed soon, and he prayed a simple prayer from the depths of his being: "'My soul is crushed with grief.' . . . He went on a little farther and bowed with his face to the ground, praying, 'My

Father! If it is possible, let this cup of suffering be taken away from me'" (Matthew 26:38-39).

Jesus' other anxious moment of prayer was during his crucifixion. He was in pain and lonely. Suffering and exhausted, he shouted, "My God, my God, why have you abandoned me?" (Matthew 27:46). Instead of crying out in his own words, he quoted Psalm 22, which is a Hebrew song written to be prayed during times of anguish.

Both these moments show Jesus using an ancient form of prayer called a *lament*. Lament prayers are emotionally honest prayers that invite us to use whatever words we need to express what we are feeling. They are messy, raw prayers, and they show that God can handle our thoughts and feelings. They are also self-compassionate prayers because they remind us it's okay to be honest with God.

When I'm anxious, I will sometimes pray lament prayers. I trust that I can tell God exactly what I am feeling, even when it sounds muddled and full of doubt. Again, the goal of prayer is not to gain absolute certainty or shut down anxious thoughts. Lament invites us to acknowledge our doubts and fears while remembering that we are deeply loved.

ACTION STEPS

1. *Pray the Lord's Prayer this week.* Try it the way it is written. Consider writing it in your own words. Between each line, stop and silently reflect on how what you are praying helps you to be closer to God and others. When you finish the prayer, tell yourself that God is pleased with what you have done (even if it doesn't match your thoughts and feelings). You prayed the way Jesus said to pray. Embrace that.

2. *Pray a lament prayer.* Try saying something to God that you have never said to anyone. Don't hold back. If you struggle with this, consider writing a lament prayer. Start with your raw

thoughts and feelings. If they express confusion or longing for something different, ask for God to do something specific, and then finish it by imagining yourself in the future when things have changed. I've included one of my lament prayers at the end of this chapter as an example.

3. *Consider praying prayers that embrace uncertainty.* A very popular prayer for people working through hardships and recovery is called the Serenity Prayer (attributed to Reinhold Niebuhr). For many years, I prayed it daily. Maybe it could help you as well.

> God, grant me the serenity to accept the things I cannot change, the courage to change the things I can, and the wisdom to know the difference.
>
> Living one day at a time, enjoying one moment at a time; accepting hardship as a pathway to peace; taking, as Jesus did, this sinful world as it is, not as I would have it, trusting that you will make all things right if I surrender to your will; so that I may be reasonably happy in this life and supremely happy with you in the next. Amen.

Creating a Lament Prayer

Most of my lament prayers are spontaneous, but to help me express all that I am feeling, I use a simple acrostic that is based on the common elements of lament prayers in the Psalms:

- **L**ay out your problem.
- **A**llow your emotions to flow.
- **M**ake your request.
- **E**xamine yourself.
- **N**ote God's past work.
- **T**rust in God's faithfulness.

A lament prayer.

God, I'm coming to you again with the same stuff. My brain is spinning out of control. I'm anxious about so many things that I can't even stop to name them individually. I'm just so stressed right now. I'm disappointed in myself for not being more in control, I feel like your patience for me is wearing thin, and I also feel guilty for thinking that way about you. I'm just so tired of these negative thoughts and feelings.

God, help me right now. Bring a hard stop to the worry loops in my brain, or just remind me that you are right with me in them. Don't let me get buried by all these thoughts, and protect me from the unhealthy ways I try to get rid of them. I know I haven't been getting the sleep I need, and that's adding to the problem. I'm also slipping back into my "if I just try harder, I don't need anyone's help" way of thinking, so I've kind of isolated myself. But I know I'm more honest with you and myself than I've ever been, so I'm doing better than before.

God, you have always gotten me through tough times. You've done it with others, you did it with Jesus, you did it with me, and you'll do it again. Sometimes you've taken longer than I've wanted, but I tend to learn things even in those situations. I don't know what you're going to do next, but I want to stick close to you, because I know you love me. I know I can't trust that things will turn out like I want—or expect—but I trust you. So, help me to focus less on the outcome and more on who I am becoming by being closer to you. Thank you. Amen.

7

Take Care of Your Whole Self

Anxiety may not completely disappear,
but eating right, sleeping well, exercising,
and caring for your soul will reduce
its control over your life.

TAKE A HIKE ... it's only 2,744 steps!" That's how Manitou Springs advertises the Incline, their recreational hiking trail on the eastern flank of Pikes Peak in Colorado. It climbs over two thousand vertical feet in less than a mile, with sections as steep as 68-percent grade.

"It's only 2,744 steps!" is also how my friend, a seasoned hiker and outdoorsman, pitched it to me and a group of guys planning to meet in Colorado.

"Do you work out?' he asked.

"No," I replied.

"Do you run?" he asked.

"Only when chased," I said with a smirk.

"Well," he said, "start taking care of yourself and do some walking and jogging to build your stamina. I think you can do the Incline. It'll be great."

That invitation began a unique season in my life. I began looking at my overall health—body, soul, and mind. I discovered that many of my struggles with anxiety were linked to an imbalance in one or more of these three areas.

Some people have struggled for years believing that the answer to anxiety is "thinking right." But anxiety isn't all in our heads—because *we* aren't all in our heads! We are wonderfully and intimately woven together as complete human beings.

Anxiety is a complex reaction to our surroundings that involves all we are—from our bodily organs like our brain and heart, to our habits like eating, drinking, digestion, and sleep, to our spiritual and mental well-being, including our core beliefs and values, friendships, and self-talk.

Eating and drinking. In preparing for the Incline, I started an eating program that including smaller, balanced meals throughout the day. I also upped my water intake; I realized I'd been overeating for years because I'd confused hunger with thirst. Changing my eating and hydration habits helped me focus and feel better. Having a balanced diet, staying hydrated, and generally avoiding things like alcohol and caffeine can have tremendous effects on our anxiety. Staying hydrated and slowly metabolizing carbohydrates can also help maintain blood sugar levels, helping us to feel calmer.

Sleep. I've snored for years. After completing a sleep study, I found out I have sleep apnea. I began using a CPAP machine, and in a couple of months, I had more energy and my mood was better. I believe some of my anxiety and depression resulted from being sleep deprived.

Rest. Sleep is important, but so is rest. Rest is a sense of calm and inactivity in our waking hours. Good sleep and rest are directly connected to calming our anxious minds. We need to make sleep and rest a priority. This may include exercising and avoiding long naps so we are fully tired by the day's end, which will help us with insomnia.

Digestion and gut health. We are only starting to discover how important our digestive system is to our overall health. Experts now believe that most of the body's serotonin (the neurotransmitter responsible for feelings of contentment and happiness) is made in the linings of the digestive tract. Harvard School of Medicine has recognized the growing field of nutritional psychiatry, which has discovered how irritation in the bowels and digestive tract can send signals to the brain, causing mood changes. Improving our gut health can help with anxiety.

Brain health. Our brains are complex organs that contain four chemicals that can improve our mood: dopamine, endorphins, oxytocin, and serotonin. New thinking and behavior can stimulate these God-given chemicals and, if needed, there are simple medications that prolong the presence of these chemicals in our brains. My friend Chris, the clinical director of a counseling center, helped my wife and me in our thinking about medications by comparing them to water wings for swimming. Sometimes people need them long term, but they are often a temporary help until we can learn new skills.

Spiritual disciplines and serving others. Someone once asked Jesus, "What is the greatest commandment in the Bible?" In his normal way of not answering questions as they were asked, he said, "There are two. Love God with all your heart, mind, soul, and strength. And love your neighbor as yourself" (see Matthew 22:34-40). Anxiety can be very self-absorbing. To live the rich and meaningful life intended for us, Jesus invites us to look up to God and out to others. Continuing to develop our spiritual lives through prayer, reading, singing, and serving others can help us with our anxiety.

How are you doing with taking care of your whole self?

Maybe you've been dealing with your stress by working a lot, and finding a way to sleep better or rest more would be helpful. Maybe your diet isn't the best it could be. This isn't about being your ideal weight or comparing yourself to others. It's about gratefully caring for the body God has given you. Maybe some medications can help you stay "above the water line" as you learn new healthy habits. Or maybe there's a deeper spiritual longing in your life. This could be a time to revisit your relationship with God and church.

Before we go any further, let's pause and celebrate.

You've completed seven sections of this field guide!

I want you to hear this loud and clear: you can do it!

Anxiety is tough, and you have a lot of courage. You might not feel like you've gotten very far, but you are on your way. Whether this is your first book about anxiety or your hundredth, it also takes a lot of courage to pick up a book and get this far. Way to go!

By the way—I did the Manitou Incline! It was brutal, but I made it. Preparing for those 2,744 steps did wonders for me physically, emotionally, and spiritually. It also helped me take new steps with my anxiety.

ACTION STEPS

1. *Get a checkup from your doctor.* Get a full physical by a physician. Identify one area to improve your physical health and create one positive and achievable goal. For example, "I am going to allow myself only a few sugary drinks each week" or "I am going to lower my cholesterol by my next appointment." Also, many doctor visits now include assessments for depression and anxiety. If one is not included, ask for one. This was very helpful to me.

2. *Begin one activity to help you get physical exercise.* We were created to be physically active. Exercise increases certain "happy chemicals" in our brains. I believe the release of serotonin in our brain is our Creator's way of saying "you're welcome" for living healthily in the world. Exercise can also get you back on normal sleep schedules by appropriately wearing you out. Choose something simple and doable. I decided to take a twenty-minute walk every evening. This helped me reduce times of anxiety late at night.

3. *Get involved in church.* If you're not connected to a church, find one that does their best to explain how to live out Jesus' teachings in practical ways and get involved. Learn more about God and the Bible, sing and worship with others, build new relationships, and volunteer where needed. Nurturing your relationship with God and serving others are essential to what it means to be complete in Christ. The apostle John wrote, "Dear friend, I hope all is well with you and that you are as healthy in body as you are strong in spirit" (3 John 2).

8

See Worry as a Gift

Worry is something that takes a lot of energy,
but it can be useful. Instead of trying
to get rid of it, you can turn worry
into something positive.

REMEMBER THE FIRST TIME I performed on a stage in middle school. Everyone in our drama class had to act out a short scene and then get feedback on their performance. Some of you are breaking into a sweat just imagining this!

I stood on the side of the stage looking nervously at my teacher. She came over and asked, "What's wrong?"

I said, "I'm worried I'm going to mess up."

"Good," she said. "Your worry will give you just what you need to perform. Channel that fear into positive action. Use it, don't let it use you."

I did what she said. When my voice kind of cracked, I decided to speak louder and more authoritatively. When I felt jittery, I worked that nervous energy into my gestures. At one point I forgot my lines. My mind started racing, so I just grabbed onto a random thought and started making up my own lines until I found my way back to the script. It went great!

The advice my middle school drama teacher gave me to face my nervousness can be applied to anxiety too. We can turn our anxiety and fear into something good.

Worry can be a gift.

Worry (or fear) is our God-given response to threats or perceived threats. When we sense there is something to worry about, our body automatically responds and gets us ready for fight, flight, freeze, or fawn. When we face this flood of automatic responses, we can recognize it as worry and then say, "I'm going to use it instead of letting it use me."

I've used this advice for years in my job as a pastor. A lot of people think that pastors are confident, bold, and nonanxious people, but that's not true. Many of us are insecure, doubting, and hesitant, but we believe that our calling is greater than our worry.

I still experience worry all the time.

Before I walk into a hospital room of someone who is sick or dying, I get butterflies in my stomach. Before I speak at my church, my mind scrambles and goes blank. While getting ready to start a counseling appointment with someone, a little voice in my head says, "You have no idea what you're doing."

Rather than letting worry use me, I'm learning to use it. If I feel anxious about counseling someone, I'll redirect that anxiety into curiosity. I ask questions. If my mind is bouncing all over the place as I walk into a hospital visit, I will focus that nervous energy into taking a quick look around the room so I know my surroundings. If my mind goes blank as I get ready to speak in front of a group, I'll say to myself, "Well, at least I'm not on autopilot. I am right here in the moment!" That way I don't just perform what I have prepared, I try to be myself.

Increased heart rate, eyes dilating, a rush of adrenaline, and super-attentiveness (also called hypervigilance) are all attempts of the brain to worry about a threat. But let's not waste all that raw energy on worry. Let's redirect it into living our lives, because we need it! There are certain levels of mental, emotional, and physiological tension we need to excel in creativity, physical health, and our life goals. What we sometimes call worry, performance experts call "operating from optimal anxiety." Here are some examples:

Creativity. I have one friend who's an amazing musician and songwriter. He has significant struggles with anxiety. If you asked him, he would say sometimes he "needs to write." His creativity is a way for him to redirect his anxiety into something beautiful.

But something else is happening as well. I believe the reason his music and words are so beautiful is because of his anxiety! Anxiety is a call to creativity. Creative types need anxiety. Something inside them is begging to come out. They need to express themselves through words, instruments, paint, dance, or three-dimensional arts. Anxiety is a form of creative restlessness waiting to bring something new and beautiful into the world.

Physical fitness. Another friend of mine is a fitness coach. He is incredibly discerning, empathetic, and knowledgeable about the human body. He also struggles with anxiety. While exercise and good health help him with his anxiety, I believe his raw, anxious energy is what helps him excel in caring for his body.

Left unchecked, anxiety can lead to exercise addiction, eating disorders, or body worship. But if we invite God into our worry, our restlessness can be transformed into loving God with our mind, body, and spirit, as well as taking care of ourselves so we can be more available for God.

Life goals. I had been feeling antsy and preoccupied with this whole topic of anxiety in my life. I'd been waking up thinking about it, where God is in it, and how I could help others with what I am learning. I finally said, "I'm going to write a book about it." I took my worry about anxiety and put it into a life goal to help others. What if that raw energy you currently call "worry" could be redirected into a larger goal that can honor God and help others?

Worry is directionless energy looking for purpose. It's your brain and body saying, "I'm ready—but I don't know what for!" You can give your worry a purpose. Worry can be a gift that prepares you for your calling, purpose, and opportunities.

ACTION STEPS

1. *Become more aware of your moments of worry.* Pay more attention this week to your thoughts, feelings, and surroundings. See if you can notice when you're starting to get worried about something. What is happening around you? What are you thinking? What are you feeling? If you've created a mood log, write these observations down there.

2. *Reframe your worry with different language.* Instead of seeing worry as a negative thing, see it as an essential energy for getting things done. Instead of calling it worry, you could call it "creative energy." The physical sensations you associate with worry may be God-given gifts that are preparing you for action. The goal here is to start removing the guilt and shame about your worry. Ask yourself, "How can I use this nervous energy for good?"

3. *Redirect your worry into a God-honoring activity.* Find an activity that can better utilize the energy you give to worry. Maybe it's a creative hobby, or a physical activity, or making a plan to complete a goal. Don't simply use this activity as a distraction from your worries. See it as an important way for you to use your nervous energy for something good, empowering, and life-giving to others.

9

Know Your Triggers

You have unique ways your anxiety is triggered.
Knowing your triggers can empower you
to change your responses.

I HAVE A LITTLE WORKSHOP in my garage. Sometimes in the middle of a sleepless night, I'll sneak downstairs to the garage to work on projects. If I forget to turn off our home alarm, when I open the door to the garage, the alarm gets triggered. The alarm starts with a soft beeping, and a soothing voice says, "Disarm system." If I don't get to it quickly, it turns into a blaring alarm and a stronger voice.

Knowing what triggers the alarm is important.

It's a good metaphor for the threat center in our brains. The threat center is designed to trigger when there might be an unexpected intruder posing a threat. What triggers the alarm, what it sounds like, and the message we hear when the alarm goes off are different for each one of us.

In my interactions with people, I have noticed four common areas that can trigger anxiety.

1. Money: losing a job, taking on debt, filing taxes, creating a budget, keeping a budget, unexpected bills, increase or decrease in income

2. People: fear of disappointing others, social embarrassment, stress of family gatherings, loss of a family member, arrival of a new family member, anticipating difficult conversations

3. Health: fear of getting sick or contaminated by something, getting a new diagnosis, complications of an existing condition, changes in emotions or mood that could point to an underlying mental health struggle

4. Faith: fear of offending God or losing faith, questioning meaning or purpose, religious guilt or shame, regret about sin, lack of connection with God, a new sense of calling

We will likely encounter all these events at some time or another. Maybe you can relate to these or have other ones that come to mind.

We may also experience multiple triggers at once. For example, an upcoming holiday could trigger anxiety regarding money, people, health, and faith.

Anxiety isn't just about bad things. Good things can trigger anxiety as well. The arrival of a new baby can be just as anxiety producing as the loss of a parent.

Sometimes our past experiences cause our triggers to be linked to internal messages in our minds. For example, a child who was called "stupid" when she dropped things could grow up hearing that word in her mind when making mistakes as an adult. Like my home alarm system, these internal messages can be soft or loud. Here are some examples:

- "You did something wrong."

  soft: concern that you made an irreversible mistake or that you offended or harmed someone

  loud: excessive worrying about your self-worth, negative ruminating, fatalistic thinking

- "You'd better check that."

  soft: a sense that you've not completed a task

loud: an intrusive need for counting or recounting, locking or unlocking doors, turning lights on or off

- "You're not clean."

  soft: a sense that you are unclean, contaminated, or vulnerable to sickness—outside or inside

  loud: an intrusive urge to repeatedly wash your hands, excessively clean surfaces, or get checked

- "You better not get rid of that."

  soft: indecision or disorganization about possessions

  loud: inability to let go of possessions, hoarding, hiding, and isolating from embarrassment

- "You can't handle that sound (or feeling)."

  soft: discomfort or annoyance with sounds

  loud: hyperawareness of or intolerance to people talking, chewing, swallowing, or moving

For those of us with obsessive-compulsive disorder, these messages can lead to what's called a *spike*. A spike is when a trigger and a need to perform something to eliminate it occur so close together that they feel like one instantaneous event.

Knowing your triggers is important in finding freedom from anxiety. A great example of this just happened to me. While writing this chapter, my computer crashed. I lost about an hour of work. (What you're now reading is a rewrite.) I can get easily confused and frustrated with my computer. Because I am not very technologically savvy, technology can be a trigger for me.

When the computer crashed, I had a spike of unwanted thoughts and feelings. Self-condemning messages flooded my brain: "You did something wrong. You should have backed things up in three places, not just two. You should have been more prepared." Then my body started responding as well. I got antsy, easily distracted, and suddenly craved food (which is one way I've learned to un-healthily self-soothe). After a few minutes of pacing and lamenting, I realized I was having a spike.

I used to rage and then withdraw into depression when I'd lose what I'd written. Not anymore. I've learned that there's always a risk of technology failing. Now I tell myself, "If I can't get the file back, maybe I have something better to write the second time." I look at the lost file as a discarded first draft. That's how I manage this kind of spike.

At this point you might be thinking, *This is great! Knowing my triggers and spikes will help me better avoid them, right?*

Wrong. Knowing your triggers and spikes will help you spot them so you can face them, tolerate the anxiety they bring, and retrain your brain to respond differently.

You are reading this book because you have given in to your fears instead of facing them. Your anxiety has grown because you've avoided what you fear. You've believed the "bully in your brain." How do you defeat a bully? You stand up to him or her. We'll explore this more in the next section.

ACTION STEPS

1. *Build a fear ladder.* Make a list of a few actions, situations, objects, or people that bring you anxiety. For example: parties, making mistakes, deadlines, catching an illness, and so on. List them in order of intensity. Under each one, write down three specific ways they bring you anxiety and rank them in intensity. For example, "making mistakes" may be your main source of anxiety. Under that you might have "showing up late" (4), "wearing the wrong clothes" (1), "forgetting some-one's birthday" (7). I've included my own fear ladder at the end of this chapter as an example.

2. *Write out your anxious messages.* Next to each thing you fear, write the internal message you hear when you think about

that source of anxiety. For example, if you have a fear of elevators, you might write, "You're going to be trapped forever," or "The elevator is going to fall to the ground." Maybe note, too, whether the message is soft or loud. Next time you get anxious, recognize the internal message and gently start to question its truthfulness. The goal is not to silence, extinguish, or dismiss the message. This can make the message louder. Just begin by doubting its accuracy.

3. *Look for predictable patterns.* Compare your fear ladder to your mood log. When are you likely to experience triggers or spikes in your anxiety? What potential anxious moments can you begin to anticipate in your daily, weekly, and monthly schedule, and your yearly routines? Again, you are not looking for what to avoid but how to better prepare to face your fears.

Table 9.1. Fear ladder

Action/Situation/Object/People	Fear Rating (10 being most fearful)
1. Financial security/safety	
Having no savings	9
Being in debt	8
Holiday shopping	8
Charitable giving/tithing	1
2. Disappointing people	
Hurting people's feelings	8
Having unresolved conflicts	7
Appearing unprepared or lazy	6
Needing to apologize	1
3. Social interactions	
Showing up on time	8
Large social gatherings	7
Meeting new people	4
One-on-one conversations	1

4. Being organized	
Having things "in their place"	7
People judging me as messy	7
Having things straight/in order	5
Being "presentable" for guests	3
5. Being clean	
Having body/mouth odor	5
Having marks or blemishes	3
Appearing unkept	2
Being in dirty places	1

10

Engage, Don't Avoid

Anxiety grows through avoidance.
You can get healthier by exposing yourself to your fears,
working with feelings that come with them,
and retraining your brain to respond differently.

I N 2010, MY WIFE and I took our three kids on a road trip through some tourist sites in the American Southwest. We went to Las Vegas, the Grand Canyon, the Hoover Dam, and Bryce Canyon, and we finished our trip in Sedona, Arizona. We found a great place near Sedona called Slide Rock State Park. It's named for moss-covered rocks that form a natural water slide. We spent the day sunning and sliding in a river, surrounded by the beautiful red rocks of Sedona.

At the end of the day, we floated down a small stream to a large open area under a bridge. We found people jumping off three rock cliffs—one was about ten feet high, the other was twenty-five feet, and the highest was fifty feet. The five of us sat on the rocks nearby and watched risk-takers leap into the air and splash into the water.

Our ten-year-old son said he wanted to try the ten-foot jump. He got up the courage and did it! Then he convinced himself to do the twenty-five-foot jump—and he did that too! I was inspired. In a rare moment of impulsiveness, I said to my wife, "Let's jump off that fifty-foot cliff!" In an equally rare moment, she said okay. And in what was probably our worst parenting moment, we left our cold, wet, under-aged children with complete strangers sitting on the rocks below (far from home) to watch their parents leap off a fifty-foot cliff.

We climbed a steep path to the top, where we found a guy coaching people on how to jump. Here's what he told us: "Walk to the edge, choose a spot in the water, then count to three and jump. Don't spend time thinking about it. If you overthink it, you'll talk yourself out of it. There are a bunch of people sitting there waiting to 'feel ready enough' to jump. That feeling will never come. Have fun, it's gonna be great!"

We did as we were told. We held hands, walked to the edge, looked down, counted to three, and jumped.

We did it!

When we got out of the water, those anxious people were still sitting at the top of the cliff. Their anxiety grew the longer they waited. They were still there when we left Slide Rock State Park. Maybe they're still there!

Those anxious people illustrate an important truth we must understand: anxiety grows stronger with avoidance.

We are always searching for the feeling of readiness or certainty, but often we never get it. So we don't act. We don't speak up for ourselves. We don't ask that person out on a date. We don't try that new activity. We don't challenge that idea at work. We aren't honest with our spouse (or ourselves). We don't stand up to the bully. And we don't have fun.

We convince ourselves that avoidance is being safe and smart, but we know that we are missing out on living. Those of us with chronic worry, intrusive thoughts, and unwanted feelings need to learn to push through false alarms in our brains and take risks. We need to face our fears. This is one of the four principles I introduced in the beginning of the field guide: exposure. Exposure is when you understand your fears and begin facing them rather than avoiding them.

When your brain sends you the signal to be afraid, it's looking for confirmation. It's trying to warn you of potential danger, but it's not totally sure. It says, "This is something to be afraid of . . . right?" Your actions confirm or question that danger signal, and your brain learns from that. When you push through your anxiety, your brain says, "Hmm, maybe that isn't something to be afraid of next time." When you avoid, your brain says, "I was right! This is something we should keep being anxious about."

For example, my wife has always had a fear of spiders. She'd always say, "I can't even look at them! I can't do it." So during my anxiety counseling, I asked if she'd also try slowly and intentionally facing her fear of spiders through exposure, and we could talk each other through those feelings. She agreed. She started with looking at pictures of spiders; she'd allow herself to get anxious and process those feelings. And you know what, it worked! I was so proud of her for facing her fear. These days she's not exactly cuddling up with spiders, but she doesn't get triggered, go into a panic, and get overcome with anxiety anymore. I'm hoping to see her one day holding a big, gnarly, hairy spider.

The emotions of fear, anxiety, and worry are part of how God has hardwired our brains, but our responses to these emotions are mostly learned—and God can help us respond in new ways. They are learned responses—which means we can relearn them. This is part of the neuroplasticity of our brains. Avoidance reinforces anxiety; engagement through exposure helps us retrain ourselves to be less anxious in the future.

You might be thinking, "But that spider could hurt her!" Absolutely! Engagement through exposure is not about eliminating all uncertainty. Let me go back to the story of Marie and me jumping off the cliff. When we hit the water, Marie's legs were slightly spread apart, and I was looking down. She bruised her tailbone and I broke some blood vessels in my eye.

The point of that story is not, "If you push through your anxiety, nothing bad will happen." The point is that your fears have kept you paralyzed. Pushing through your fears will help you live the life you're meant to live. The more you avoid, the more your anxiety grows. I'm not recommending jumping off cliffs . . . well, maybe I am. I am inviting you to leap from the safety and security of your fears into the refreshing waters that life is offering you.

In the previous section, I asked you to create a mood log and a fear ladder. If you haven't done that yet, take some time and start on these. They don't have to be perfect or even complete, but you'll be using them more as you move ahead.

ACTION STEPS

1. *Expose yourself to something on your fear ladder.* Find the fear with the lowest ranking number and gently try to face that fear directly. For example, if you have a fear of speaking in public, try speaking up in a social setting, like a small group or a class. If that's too much, start exposing yourself to the idea of talking in public. Imagine speaking up in a social setting, let yourself feel some of the anxiety that idea brings, and then use some of the *Anxiety Field Guide* tools you've learned to respond differently to your thoughts and feelings.

2. *Experience the feelings.* Before, during, and after you do what you feared, examine your thoughts and feelings. Write them in your mood log. This is important. You may want to say, "I did it. I don't want to think about it anymore," but that's also a form of avoidance. Don't try to avoid your thoughts and feelings. Experience them and write them down.

3. *Celebrate the success.* If you took a small step toward your fears and documented some of your anxious thoughts and feelings—congratulations! You did it! You've started courageously and thoughtfully engaging your anxiety. Whether you found it easy or distressing, this is the way forward. Take a moment and celebrate that you can keep going. There is hope.

11

Focus Forward

Anxiety grows as you focus on it.
Acknowledging the anxiety and then focusing on
what is more important will help you
prevent "anxiety crashes."

I **WAS DRIVING DOWN** the 405 freeway on my way to an appointment. The freeway was wide open, but I noticed some sirens on the left shoulder ahead of me. There was an accident.

I looked out my window and slowed down. They call this *rubbernecking,* and I'm an expert rubbernecker. I was doing my own little drive-by investigation. I examined the damage to the cars, found the drivers the police were speaking with, and imagined how the accident happened. Then suddenly—AAAAAGH!

I was so distracted by the accident that I hadn't seen the car in front of me! I slammed on the brakes and stopped an inch from rearending the car. This happened right in front of the accident site. I breathed a sigh of relief and then slowly looked over to the police officer investigating the accident. He gave me a knowing glance as if to say, "Yup, that's how this happens."

What happened? I was so focused on the bad stuff that I almost crashed. I thought, *That's a picture of worry.* When I spend too much time focusing on the bad things, I'm more likely to have "anxiety crashes."

Anxiety feeds off attention. The more attention we give to our worries, the more powerful they become. It's not bad enough that we have sirens going off in our heads: there are also sirens all around us. We live in a world focused on bad things. We are always reminded of things to worry about. We want to ignore the things that worry us, but that doesn't work, because anxiety also grows through avoidance. So we're stuck! Anxiety grows through attention and avoidance. What can we do?

A simple technique to help us with our anxiety is a middle ground between attention and avoidance. Let me explain it by going back to that story of my near accident on the freeway.

I could have avoided the near-collision two ways. First, I could have just ignored looking at the accident altogether. If I had never looked to my left, I would have seen the car in front of me. Simple, but not realistic. I am a curious person. It's natural to look. It's not wrong. Second, I could have also just stopped the car and given the accident my full attention. No movement, no collision. That's not realistic either.

But there's a third way: look at the collision for a moment, acknowledge it, gather some information, and then get my eyes back on the road ahead where they belong!

My counselor, Scott Symington, taught me this technique in dealing with my anxiety. It's called the Two-Screen Method. Scott explains it in detail in his book *Freedom from Anxious Thoughts and Feelings*, which I've also included in the recommended resources section at the end of this book.

Here's the basic idea: Imagine a TV screen in front of you. On that screen are the good things God wants you to look at: your family, your job, your school, your values, your areas of growth and opportunity, and the people in your life who help you to move forward in healthy ways. There are challenges and conflicts, but they are good growth areas for you.

Now imagine that there's another screen in your peripheral vision. This side screen displays all kinds of things—all of the problems in the world, other people's bad choices, people's opinions of you, current and upcoming events you cannot control, the mistakes you've made, and the past successes you wish you had now. This screen begs for your full attention.

Rather than giving that side screen your full attention or ignoring it all together, you can look at it, acknowledge it, gather some information from it, and then focus back on the front screen, where your attention belongs. When we are anxious, this simple technique of looking briefly to the side and then back to the front can help us prevent "anxiety crashes."

That side screen (or my car's window in my story) can be alluring. The sirens in our brain are sending us a message that we should focus all our attention on what's over there! That's probably the same thinking that led to the crash on the freeway.

Here's an example of how I used this technique with an anxiety of mine—reading and answering negative emails. The other night I got an email from someone accusing me of doing something wrong. The person also attributed some terrible motives to me. In the past, I would have had one of two reactions: I'd try to completely ignore the email, or I would give it my absolute full attention, investing more time and energy than is healthy.

The Two-Screen Method says, "Allow yourself to see and acknowledge the source of your anxiety and then gently redirect the focus of your attention back to what deserves your attention at this moment." So I tried that.

I read the email and said to myself, "Wow, that email stings. I feel defensive. I want to correct this person, but I also wonder if I did do something wrong. I think I need to give this some more attention when I'm not so emotionally confused and anxious. I don't need to respond right away." I then went back to what I was doing before I read the email. I still felt anxiety, but I had a plan.

That's the first step: accept and redirect.

But redirect to what? Redirect back to the front screen, which will be different for each one of us. It might be our current responsibilities at the time (working, family, or hobbies) or positive ways of thinking (our core beliefs, values, and spiritual worldview). It could also be redirecting our attention to a time and place where we can give our anxiety our full attention. We'll address this in the next section. I've found that simply giving myself permission to acknowledge my anxiety without focusing on it is a healthy redirection that keeps me focusing forward.

This redirection technique is a new way of expressing ancient wisdom. In his last piece of guidance to anxious Jesus-followers in his day, the apostle Paul describes redirection like this: "And now, dear brothers and sisters, one final thing. Fix your thoughts on what is true, and honorable, and right, and pure, and lovely, and admirable. Think about things that are excellent and worthy of praise" (Philippians 4:8).

ACTION STEPS

1. *Make a list of what deserves your focus.* Examine your life and write down the good, purposeful, and life-giving people, activities, and ideas that help you focus forward. It can be important relationships, meaningful work, creative hobbies, and truths about your identity. For example, I believe that I am loved, forgiven, and gifted by God for good things in this world. This belongs on my "front screen." When that side screen says, "You're an idiot," I can redirect my focus to what God thinks of me.

2. *Practice the Two-Screen Method.* In your next anxious moment, don't avoid or give your full attention to what is making you anxious. Accept and redirect. Acknowledge your anxious thoughts and feelings, give yourself a few moments, and then focus on something more deserving of your attention. If it helps you, decide on a time in your schedule when you can

revisit those anxious thoughts or feelings to process them in a different way.

3. *Reduce "feeding your side screen."* Recognize and reduce content that will unnecessarily trigger you. For example, spend less time checking news sites, scanning social media, listening to negativity, or revisiting conversations in your head. You don't want to avoid what triggers you, but limit your exposure to things that will make it harder to get well.

12

Put Time Limits on Your Worry

Anxiety demands immediate action.
Take the power back by deciding when, where,
and for how long you will worry.

HAVE A FRIEND WHOSE TEN-YEAR-OLD daughter struggles with worry. She would often come home from school with many things weighing her down. The evenings were especially difficult for her. As the sun began to set, she would feel she had less time to think about all the issues that concern her. She usually lost her appetite for dinner, locked herself in her room to try and focus, and stayed up late to complete her homework. The next day she would be sleep deprived, which only added to her challenges.

But she and her mom ended up reading about an idea that almost immediately changed their situation for the better—Create a Worry Box: Find a small box to put in your room. Decorate it in a way that is meaningful to you. When you have a worry, concern, or source of anxiety, write it on a piece of paper as a note to yourself. Put that note in the worry box and then go back to your day. Then each day, take a note out of the box. Read it and give your attention to it. If your worry diminishes, you may choose to throw away the note. If you feel like there is more to worry about, put it back in the box to look at another time.

It worked!

My friend's daughter had a breakthrough. Her emotional life and time management changed. She was able to get her homework done earlier, get to bed at a reasonable time, and even get her evening appetite back!

A worry box isn't magic. It also didn't cure her anxiety. A worry box is a simple technique that creates opportunities to put some important skills into practice, skills like normalization, awareness, and exposure. Most importantly, a worry box is about putting time limits on your worry. When we limit the attention we give to anxiety, it can minimize the powerful influence it has on our lives.

Here's how a creating a worry box can help you find freedom from chronic worry, intrusive thoughts, and unwanted feelings.

A worry box allows anxiety to have a place in our lives. As we've already learned, anxiety is normal and necessary. It's a God-given response to a perceived threat. We shouldn't fight it, ignore it, or try to extinguish it. Think of anxiety like having a dog in your home. You want it to be a good companion and warn you of real threats, but you can't let it chew the furniture and pee everywhere. There's a place for anxiety in our lives, but it needs training and boundaries.

A worry box is a way of saying, "I can give my worry a welcoming and beautiful place, but it needs to be limited." My friend's daughter created a pretty box for her worry. It was a five-inch cube made of cardboard. It was colorful and fun to look at. It matched her room nicely, and unless you knew the story, you'd never know what it was for.

A worry box gives us control over our worry. Anxiety is an automatic response of the brain and body that makes us feel out of control. The good news is, we are not our brains. We can interrupt anxiety's control and take responsibility for what we do with our thoughts and feelings.

The apostle Paul wrote in the New Testament, "We take captive every thought to make it obedient to Christ" (2 Corinthians 10:5 NIV). He's saying that there are thoughts and ways of seeing things that can lead us away from the good life we are meant to live. A worry box is a way for us to say, "I have anxiety, and I can choose when, where, and how I will deal with it."

A worry box allows some worries to not be resolved. Anxiety demands closure, but many things in life don't have closure. Relationships are not tidy, communication can be vague, and the future is unknowable. Life is full of uncertainty and mystery. A worry box is a physical reminder that we can live full and meaningful lives while still allowing anxiety to exist.

We will always have things in our worry box. It's our way of saying, "I don't have an answer for that worry yet. And that's okay." Worry boxes are a way to practice something called *systematic desensitization*. By allowing our worries to remain, we are retraining ourselves to be able to tolerate uncertainty.

Probably the most important part of using a worry box is practicing self-control when we open it. A worry box can become a Pandora's box, exploding a world of anxiety onto you! My friend's daughter was instructed to only allow about ten minutes a day for "active worrying." Again, the goal here is not to eliminate your worry. That may never happen. The goal here is to give some time to worry and then move on with the rest of your life.

You might be wondering, *Do I need an actual box? Can't I do this in my head?* Some people find that the physical object of a box, with actual pieces of paper, activates areas of their brain in ways that help them immensely. Personally, I use the idea of a worry box as a mental exercise. In fact, as I started writing this section, this anxious thought popped into my brain: *I don't think I know enough about this subject to write about it.* I took about ten seconds and then thought, *That might be true. Let me make a mental note of that worry, write what I do know about this subject, and then I'll get back to that worry when*

I'm done writing. By the time I finished writing this section, I went back to think about that worry and decided I could discard it.

ACTION STEPS

1. *Create a worry box.* Decide if you would like a physical or mental worry box. Consider activating your creative side by making something physical. I have a friend who does woodworking. He created a beautiful wood box for this. The experience of making it was very therapeutic. If it is physical, find a place for it in your life that will make it easily accessible to you. Make it nice. It's not a bad box. It's designed to honor an important part of you that needs some boundaries.

2. *Put your worries in the worry box.* When you have a worry or anxiety, make a note for yourself and put it in the box. If you are not near it, put the note somewhere that will act like the box until you can put it there. You may want to reread what was said about the Two-Screen Method. A worry box is a physical way to apply this technique. Accept the anxiety by writing it down and putting it aside. Then redirect yourself back to what is most important. I have a digital worry box on my phone, a notes app where I log things to think about later.

3. *Choose the right time to worry.* Find a time and place to revisit your worries. I would suggest drawing notes from the box without looking. This helps you have less of an agenda. You might discover previous worries that can be discarded. Also, you might ask a trusted friend to help you process your worries. Their questions and affirmations may help you avoid unhealthy cycles of anxious ruminating.

13

Speak Kindly to Yourself

*Your internal dialogue can alleviate
or aggravate your anxious moments.
Rather than being self-condemning,
you can learn to be gracious with yourself.*

O NE OF MY MENTAL ACTIVITIES when I was a kid was inter-viewing myself. I would imagine myself on a late-night talk show. The host would say, "My guest tonight is a great young man. He's most known for [then I'd insert whatever great accomplishment I'd dreamed of that week]." Then the host would say, "Let's welcome . . . Jason Cusick!"

I'd step out from behind the curtain as the band would start to play. I'd give the band leader a little head nod. As the audience ap-plauded, I'd wave to the three sections of people in their seats. Then I'd step up on the little platform. The host would come around the desk, shake my hand, and pull me in a little to say something in my ear. We'd both smile as I'd sit down. We'd have a little small talk and then the host would ask, "So, Jason . . . what's new?"

When these interviews played out in my imagination, the host was always interested in what I was doing. He'd say things like, "Wow, tell me more about that!" He was also always affirming. He'd say, "I saw what you did. You're really talented." He had good questions too, like, "What do you mean by that?"

He was a great host! He should be. I mean, he was me, right? All those imagined interviews were me interviewing myself. Those interviews were interesting, affirming, and self-clarifying. But for other conversations in my head, that wise host was absent.

During those times I'd say to myself, "You're not good enough. Your ears are too big. You have too many freckles. You should have [insert whatever I felt like I should have done]." These inner criticisms weren't constant, but they showed up at the exact times when they could be most damaging.

How we talk to ourselves and about ourselves is incredibly important in finding freedom from anxiety. Our greatest battles are won and lost in the mind.

For those of us living with anxiety, it's difficult to capture our negative self-talk and expose its lies. This is because our negative self-talk is disguised in our own voice. We have learned to trust ourselves. When we think or feel something, we believe it comes from the best, most rational, and truest part of ourselves. But that is not always the case.

I have a friend I'll call Claire. She's struggled with mental illness for most of her life. She has depression, self-harm behaviors, and crippling low self-image. Her physical appearance always matched her mental condition. She was often unkept, haggard, and isolated.

I remember visiting her at different psychiatric facilities where she'd voluntarily checked herself in. Many of her problems were rooted in her ongoing battle with schizophrenia, a condition that causes disordered thinking, delusions, and hallucinations. Claire struggled with a common symptom of schizophrenia: hearing self-destructive voices in her head.

I saw Claire recently, and she was a changed woman! She was wearing a new outfit and smiling as she spoke to someone at church. In a private moment, I shared what I noticed about her. She blushed and then said, "I found a new medication that really helps me. It might not be permanent, but it's helping for now."

"Are the voices gone?" I asked.

"Oh! No," she said. "I'm just learning not to listen to them anymore. They used to be shouts, then they became whispers, and now it's just a little mumbling in the background."

Before your anxious self says, "Maybe you have schizophrenia!" let's remember we all have "voices in our heads." The voice is ours! We all process thoughts and feelings internally throughout the day. We also do it while we sleep in ways we still don't fully understand. This is normal and natural.

But where do the negative and self-destructive thoughts and feelings inside us come from? I believe they can come from three sources: what we have told ourselves, what others have told us, and what a greater enemy of our souls wants us to believe.

What we have told ourselves. You fail a test in middle school and say to yourself, "You dummy." You didn't get that job and tell yourself, "You'll never make it." Your marriage ends and you declare, "I'm unlovable." Your brain remembers and before you know it, you have a new vocabulary of negative, self-defeating labels that evolve into your automatic thinking. The worst part is, you hear these things in your own voice!

What others have told us. Much of our self-talk comes from what we've heard from significant figures in our lives—like parents, friends, employers, or religious leaders. We were taught to trust them, but they were imperfect people and some of them have harmed us deeply. An old proverb says, "If you want a lie to seem true, say it over and over again." We may have heard negative things repeatedly, or maybe just once, and they stuck. Then we've repeated them to ourselves.

What the enemy tells us. Jesus taught that there is a personal adversary to our relationship with God: the devil, who wants to steal, kill, and destroy (John 10:10). At times, our words to ourselves are fueled by the spiritual enemy. Instead of believing his lies, Jesus invites us to believe the truth—that we are created, loved, chosen, gifted, and empowered to live the rich and meaningful life he paid for by his death and resurrection.

The next time you are calling yourself names, declaring what you can't do rather than what you can do, or you are "should-ing" all over yourself . . . speak kindly to yourself. Rather than listening to and believing the negative self-talk in your brain, interrupt it and speak something affirming and hopeful to yourself.

ACTION STEPS

1. *Pay attention to your strengths.* Make a list of your personal strengths, greatest attributes, and things you like about yourself (physically, relationally, spiritually). Instead of focusing on your weaknesses, focus on your strengths. If you feel like paying attention to your strengths seems prideful, look at them as divine gifts to be celebrated and expressed.

2. *Name the source of your negative thoughts.* The next time you have a self-condemning thought, don't try to silence it. Instead, interrogate it. Try to identify whether it's something you taught yourself to say or something someone told you that you have believed. Begin to question the truthfulness of this condemning voice or thought.

3. *Invite God's perspective into the thoughts.* When you're having anxious thoughts and feelings, invite God into that moment. Talk with God and ask him to remind you of his love for you. Our emotions are untrustworthy, and our thoughts are unreliable. But God's promises are always true.

14

Find Rest

Anxiety can starve you of a meaningful connection with your Creator, but it can also be an invitation to slow down and care for your soul.

I FELT LIKE I NEEDED a quiet place away from the busyness of my world. Someone suggested that I visit Serra Retreat House in Malibu, California, a former Catholic monastery that has been converted into a retreat center. I found the address online, put a couple of books in my car, and decided to do an all-day fast. After an early morning hour-long drive, I pulled up to the retreat house. The gate was locked. It was closed.

In my eagerness, I must have missed the part on the website about making a reservation, but I decided to wait around to see if I could get in later that day. I walked across the street and found a small grassy area with a bench overlooking the Pacific Ocean. It was quiet. The cool morning air from the beach offered an alternative way to start my day.

As I watched the waves roll in, I caught sight of something small out of the corner of my eye. It was a snail. It looked as if it was not moving at all, but it was. It was slowly creeping across the pavement and heading somewhere. I remember thinking, "At that pace, you'll be here all day." I turned my attention back to the ocean in front of me and sat in silence for what felt like a minute. I decided to look down to check the progress of my little gastropod companion. I couldn't find him! All I saw was the glittery trail of goo that snails leave behind them. "You did it!" I said. "At a snail's pace, but quicker than I thought!"

When the retreat house opened, I found I was able to spend the day there after all. It was a quiet day of rest and reflection, but I couldn't get that snail out of my mind. I drew a picture of him in the journal I'd brought with me. He became emblematic of my future visits to that retreat house and a goal for my spiritual life in general. I started to ask myself, "How can I successfully get to my destination in life without the hurry and anxiety I often carry?" and "What would it take to slow down? Do I have the nonanxious presence of that snail?"

I've discovered two practices that help me find this kind of rest: sabbath and spiritual reading. These two practices help me to slow down and find meaningful connection with my Creator. Let me share them with you.

Sabbath. The word *sabbath* refers to a day of rest. The creation story of the Hebrew Bible says that God made the world and then rested. We don't get the impression that God took this rest because he was exhausted. It appears to be a celebration and a time of reflection on the goodness of creation.

Sabbath is an invitation to follow this example of hard work followed by reflective rest. It's a gentle war against the idol of self-sufficiency. Sabbath reminds us that all good things are gifts, including our ability to work. Sabbath also cautions us against finding our identity in what we produce. We are loved, valued, and accepted not because we are hard workers but because we are created in love.

Sabbath is difficult for me. I like to be independent and often associate my value with my productivity, which makes me feel more responsible for things than I actually am. This adds to my anxiety. The first time I practiced a sabbath, I decided to nap most of the day just because this made me feel like I was "doing something."

I try to give myself one day of rest a week as well as different times of nonproductivity during the day. I find ways to slow down, breathe, and recenter myself spiritually. Lately, I have been taking leisurely walks alone, with no technology. My "solo strolls" are a way to enjoy my Creator's good world and silently be thankful for what I've been given. I try to remember Jesus' invitation to his busy and anxious disciples: "Let's go off by ourselves to a quiet place and rest awhile" (Mark 6:31).

Spiritual reading. We can practice spiritual reading with all kinds of literature, but what I'm referring to is the ancient approach to Bible reading called *lectio divina.* Many people read the Bible as an answer book for problems or a quick reference for topics. Lectio divina is an approach that invites the reader to slow down and have an encounter with the author. There are four parts to it.

The first part is called *reading,* or *lectio.* You start by finding a quiet, comfortable place to read. Choose a small section of the Bible. Read it through one time, and on this first reading, simply make observations about images, characters, and words that stand out to you. Don't force yourself to understand it.

The next part is called *reflecting,* or *meditatio.* You read the same section again and sense if you feel nudged to think more in depth about something you've read. This may involve trying to understand more about the author's meaning and message. This reflecting should include asking for divine guidance and not slipping into a purely academic study mode.

The third part is called *responding,* or *oratio.* This is when you talk with God about what you are reading and learning. This might mean praying aloud or writing your thoughts and feelings in a journal. Responding is less about what you are going to do with what you've read and more about being in conversation with your Creator, pondering what you've read.

The last part is called *rest,* or *contemplatio.* Spend ten minutes in silence. This is about allowing God to work in your heart and mind in quietness. Be open to receiving spiritual direction from God about what to do with what you have read. Your mind will wander. Don't panic. Use a notebook to jot down distracting thoughts and then gently bring your attention back to God and what you have read.

This kind of reading might seem strange or unusual to you, especially if you are new to faith. If that's true for you, consider starting with something simple and comfortable for you. The goal of these spiritual practices is to help us slow down and connect (maybe for the first time) with the One who created us. Thankfully, we can go at a snail's pace and still get there!

ACTION STEPS

1. *Spend some time alone with God.* Choose a day and location to spend time alone. I recommend a quiet outdoor place away from your normal routines. Bring something to write in and a Bible. Start your time just relaxing and being silent. Enjoy the natural world around you. When you feel ready, invite God to join you in that quietness and try some spiritual reading. You may want to consider some of the devotional resources I've recommended at the end of this book.

2. *Journal your experience.* After you've tried spending some time alone with God, write down what you experienced. Maybe nothing profoundly spiritual happened, or maybe it was a powerful experience for you. Write down your thoughts and feelings as if you were writing something to your Creator. Here's an entry from my journal: "Well, God, it was good to be quiet for a while. I don't think I got any divine revelation, but I think I needed this. I have this strange feeling that you enjoyed me being here."

3. *Separate your work from your identity.* Many of us associate who we are with what we do. We overidentify with our job, family role, or creative output. Knowing your identity apart

from your work, family, output, and appearance is important in finding rest. Make a list of who you are that is unrelated to your productivity. For example, I am a child of God, a human being, and a person loved by others. None of these things are because of what I do or don't do.

15

Look for Progress, Not Perfection

Anxiety keeps you trapped in categories of pass or fail. Learn to recognize and celebrate your progress.

I **WAS UP ALL NIGHT.** I had to have a tough conversation with someone on my leadership team the next day, and my stomach was in knots. My mind was flooded with worst-case scenarios. I found myself on a frantic search in my mind for just the right thing to say so that the conversation would end well. Nothing was working.

I started to believe that my anxious feelings were evidence that I should not have this conversation. Then the nagging, negative feeling inside me started to grow. It was accompanied by messages like, "You don't know what you're doing," and, "They should have chosen a more seasoned leader for this job."

Just then, I had a moment of clarity. I said to myself, "Oh! This is my anxiety talking."

The restlessness, the heightened sense of danger, the overthinking, the flood of negative feelings, the confusion of feelings with evidence, and the self-condemning messages—these were all signs that my brain was on overdrive, trying to protect me from a perceived threat.

Over the years I had learned a ritual to help me through these times. The ritual was overthinking. I would think long enough and eventually talk myself out of doing what I feared.

So, that night, in that moment of clarity, I realized that my anxiety was getting the best of me. I practiced some of the basic skills I had been learning:

- I quietly thanked God for a well-designed threat center in my brain.

- I accepted that no matter how much I planned, there would still be uncertainty.

- I sat back and observed these thoughts and feelings without owning them.

- I took ten seconds and identified a few of the thoughts and feelings I was having.

- I recognized that difficult conversations trigger my anxiety.

- I asked God to join me in my anxiety rather than asking for it to be supernaturally taken away.

- Finally, I resolved that the best thing I could do was to have this tough conversation, not avoid it.

The next day came. Guess what I did?

I avoided the conversation.

But I didn't see this as a failure. I saw it as progress. I had practiced a lot of helpful new skills to work through my anxious thoughts and feelings. That was reason to celebrate! I also realized that emphasizing what I didn't do, rather than focusing on what I did do, was a larger symptom of my problem with anxiety.

I believe the best part of this experience was that moment of clarity. Everything changed when I said to myself, "This is my anxiety talking!" In those few seconds, I wasn't on autopilot. I wasn't just following the preprogrammed conditioning of my anxiety.

When you feel your heart rate increase, want to avoid, have the urge to perform a ritual to make you feel better, isolate from people, or start to believe the self-condemning messages in your head, just being able to recognize these as expressions of anxiety is progress. Good job!

Someone once said, "The first step in breaking down a wall is becoming aware that the wall exists." You are coming face to face with your anxiety. You are seeing it for what it is. This is a huge step forward. Celebrate progress!

What does it look like to celebrate progress?

Think continuum, not categories. Rather than seeing things as pass or fail, we can look at our progress on a scale of one to ten. If "ten" is perfection, we can declare ten to be unattainable. If "one" is irreversible failure, we can also declare one to be impossible. That leaves us with two through nine. The question we can ask ourselves is, "How am I doing now compared to before?"

I have a friend who regularly battles negative thoughts about himself. He told me, "I have these fears that everyone hates me and I'm stuck in those thoughts for the whole day . . . sometimes more." We met together and I coached him though some of the exercises in this book. He came back to me a few weeks later and said, "I still have those negative thoughts, but now I just have them for a couple of hours, not all day." I said, "That's progress!"

Feel free to reevaluate the situation. One of the greatest disasters in maritime history is the sinking of the Titanic. There are a lot of reasons why the great "unsinkable ship" went down, but one main reason was anxiety. The investors wanted to get the new ship to its destination by a deadline (ahead of deadline, actually). This anxiety caused them to cut corners in preparation, push through conventional wisdom, and ignore warning signs. History would have been different if they had given themselves the freedom to reevaluate their situation.

My son is a driven, hardworking, responsible man. He is also a perfectionist. During one of his college years, he overcommitted himself with school and leadership responsibilities. He felt like dropping a class would be a sign of failure—but then so would failing a class. His biggest growth that year wasn't his academics but his ability to give himself permission to reevaluate his situation and drop a class. That's progress to celebrate!

Change your view of time. We have one word for time in English, but in Greek there are two words for time—*chronos* and *kairos*. *Chronos* refers to linear time: days, hours, seconds. We only have so much of this kind of time. Once *chronos* is past, it's gone. *Kairos*, on the other hand, refers to a window of opportunity or providential moment. These can happen any time, and when one passes, another will come along.

My friend Suzy has social anxiety. She learned at a young age that sharing her thoughts and feelings would lead to her being teased and rejected. As a result, she struggled to be honest in new relationships. She met a new friend and felt like she could trust and share honestly with her. It was a "*kairos* moment," but she didn't take it.

She knew she'd missed it. And just knowing that she'd missed it was progress. The next week, she saw another opportunity to share honestly. It was another "*kairos* moment." This time, she took it and shared her thoughts and feelings. That was progress too!

When I accepted the call to be the lead pastor of our church, I was flooded with anxiety. I immediately started searching the Bible for wisdom for new church leaders. I found this encouraging advice from the apostle Paul to his young protégé Timothy: "Throw yourself into your tasks so that everyone will see your progress" (1 Timothy 4:15). I decided in that moment that rather than aiming for perfection, I would learn to recognize and celebrate my progress. Maybe you could give it try. It's working for me.

ACTION STEPS

1. *Review your* **Anxiety Field Guide** *progress.* Review the table of contents of this book and celebrate what you have learned. What specific skills have you tried? Which have you incorporated into your life? How have you already seen progress in finding freedom from your anxiety?

2. *Recognize progress in others.* Choose three people in your life—like employees, family members, or friends. Write them handwritten notes and share with them the progress you see them making in areas that are important to them. As you develop a habit of celebrating progress in others, you'll be better able to do it for yourself.

3. *Form your own encouragement team.* Find two trusted friends or family members who know your struggles with anxiety. Ask them to share with you any progress they are observing in you. Have them read this book if that would help. Invite them to tell you the progress you might not be seeing.

16

Understand Obsession and Compulsion

Your first response to anxiety is to try to stop it,
but your attempts to stop it can turn into a new cycle
of avoidance. You can learn to overcome anxiety
by exhausting it through exposure.

WAS REWATCHING THE FAMOUS **1974 BOXING** match between Muhammad Ali and George Foreman. The "Rumble in the Jungle" is considered one of the greatest televised sporting matches of the twentieth century. Before the fight, Ali said he was going to win by the end of the eighth round by using a new technique called the "rope-a-dope."

In boxing, a rope-a-dope is when you allow your opponent to get you up against the ropes, cover your face, and let them swing pointless punches at your arms and body. You do what you can to get your opponent to use up all their energy while you protect yourself. Once they are exhausted, you come out fighting.

In the prefight interview, a sportscaster asked Ali, "So who is the dope?"

Ali responded, "Whoever chases me into the ropes." As he predicted, Ali knocked out Foreman in the eighth round. The last minute of that fight is a sight to see.

The rope-a-dope is an amazing boxing strategy. It's also a powerful technique to help us in our fight with anxiety.

We've learned that anxiety starts when the brain senses a perceived threat. The brain then signals the body to have automatic responses like increased heart rate, an adrenaline rush, and hypervigilance. Along with these responses, there might be intrusive thoughts or unwanted feelings—including discomfort over uncertainty, worry that you're exposed to a virus, a nagging feeling of having forgotten something, an overwhelming need for order, unwanted sexual thoughts or desire, fears of having hurt someone or offended God, or maybe the general feeling that something is just not right.

These unwanted thoughts and feelings become the focus of our attention. They preoccupy us. We can't shake them, and that bothers us. At this point, we may be having what is technically called an *obsession*. An obsession is an unwanted, intrusive thought, image, or urge that triggers intense feelings of distress.

Are you following me? Now, stick with me here on this next part.

When we get obsessions, our natural response is to try to get rid of them. We do everything to fight our obsessions—we try to minimize them, deflect them, reject them, and outthink them. When we find something that minimizes or temporarily stops the obsession, we repeat it. If it works, our brain creates an unhealthy cycle of avoidance, creating a desire to repeat whatever helped stop or relieve our obsession. We have now created what's called a *compulsion*.

Compulsions are rituals we engage in to deal with the distress of our unwanted thoughts and feelings. They are ritualized behaviors we've adopted as a way of dealing with our anxiety. They can look like normal activities to everyone else, but they have become necessary rituals for us because we are using them to try to fight our obsessions. They can be simple things like nail biting, repeating things, joking, shopping, cleaning, or exercising. They could also become things we would normally associate with obsessive-compulsive disorder like excessive hand washing, unrealistic urges to count things or have things in order, hoarding, or compulsive behaviors that require professional treatment.

Even small, innocent, and well-intentioned acts that provide a bit of relief can become compulsive if they are ritualized to deal with our unwanted thoughts and feelings. When we fight our obsessions with compulsions, we don't realize that this is getting our obsessions up against the ropes while we swing punches. Our obsessions are simply preserving strength, and we are exhausting ourselves. It's a classic rope-a-dope, and we are the dopes.

Let's apply Ali's strategy to our battle with anxiety. Rather than trying to fight our chronic worry, intrusive thoughts, and unwanted feelings, what if we let it take us to the ropes and wear itself out? What would this look like? Let me try to explain this by giving you an example from my life.

One of my biggest obsessions is about relationships. I battle with people pleasing. I will get unwanted thoughts and feelings that I have offended someone or that people don't like me, and I will believe that it's completely my responsibility to make sure all my relationships are healthy. I obsess about ensuring that my relationships are good and that people like me.

Ruminating is my compulsion. I do this by checking with people I know, seeking assurances, and overthinking my relationships. It's the way I try to fight my obsessive worry about my relationships and the opinions of others. Put another way, my compulsion is to get my relationship anxiety "against the ropes" and start punching. I have spent sleepless nights punching away my anxious feelings "against the ropes." I'm trying to knock out my anxiety, but I'm just wearing myself out.

What if instead of trying to knock out my relationship anxiety with ruminating, I let it get me against the ropes and wear itself out? Rather than fighting it, just let it keep distressing me? This is another form of "exposure." We allow ourselves to have our anxious thoughts and feelings but stay focused on the other skills we are learning, and over time, our anxious feelings begin to lose their power. It's a classic rope-a-dope, but this time, the anxiety is the dope.

I saw Ali do this in that fight. I saw him getting hit, but there was a little smile on his face the whole time. That's because he had a plan. He was accepting the blows, but he was focused on his strategy. With a strategy of protecting yourself while wearing down the power of the distressing feelings, you may be flooded with anxiety, but then, like a flood, the waters will subside.

Anxiety is a bully in your brain. I believe you can knock out anxiety, but first you must wear it down. Like George Foreman having Muhammad Ali up against the ropes, allow anxiety to swing at you over and over again. Instead of fighting it, allow it to keep coming. Feel the anxiety. Endure it. You want it to wear itself down. As you experience anxiety, don't panic. Tell yourself, "I can endure this for a little while. I'm on the ropes, but I have a plan."

While this is happening, protect yourself. Remind yourself that you are not alone. Take deep breaths and count to ten. Speak kindly to yourself. And look for progress, not perfection. You may give in so the anxiety will stop. See if you can endure your anxious thoughts and feelings for ten more seconds. That's progress!

ACTION STEPS

1. *Choose an obsession.* Identify an expression of anxiety to experiment on. Try to find a situation, action, or person that causes you anxiety but will be easy to start working on. Looking through your fear ladder and mood log can help with this.

2. *Identify the compulsion.* Do you have a behavior, ritual, or automatic response that you use to get rid of your anxiety? It may be something that seems natural or good—like thinking, praying, eating, or distracting yourself. Even though media, phone use, and social media can be for enjoyment and even

healthy distraction, they can also masquerade as compulsions and be used to avoid anxious thoughts and feelings. It could also be something people have praised you for. For me, it's humor. I crack jokes when I'm anxious. I'm learning not to avoid my anxiety through humor.

3. ***Don't do the compulsion.*** Next time you feel the anxiety that becomes an obsession, you will feel the urge to perform a compulsion to minimize your anxiety. When this happens, don't do the compulsion. Let the anxiety remain. Find something healthy to do instead (be physically active, enjoy a hobby, or spend time praying). You may end up giving in to the compulsion after some time. That's okay. Write down what you experienced and celebrate your progress.

17

Begin Exposure

You have a habit of avoiding
what brings you anxiety.
The only way to freedom
is by habitually facing what you fear.

I HAVE BAD ASTHMA.

I was hospitalized once as a child, and I had to spend a few days in an oxygen tent. The doctors ordered oxygen and steam to be pumped into the tent to help open my bronchial tubes. When I left the hospital, they told my parents that steam would help me, so my dad built a plastic tent above the shower and would tell me to take super-hot showers to create a lot of steam.

This was horrible for me as a kid. The water was so hot. I'd stand as far away from the hot water as possible, but over time I got closer and closer to it. Eventually my asthma got better, and I no longer needed the steam, but I had become used to hot showers. Now, I love hot showers. The other day I was turning down the cold water in the shower and realized it was completely off! What I used to feel as unbearably hot I learned to endure, and the more I endured it, the less it negatively affected me. I became "desensitized" to the hot water.

The same thing I learned with those showers can be applied to dealing with worry and stress. Sometimes the situations that bring us worry, anxiety, and stress can feel like scalding water. We want to get out of the water or change the temperature. It might seem counterintuitive, but the better way to deal with worry, anxiety, and stress is to learn to endure it and, over time, retrain ourselves to respond differently.

Let's connect the dots to our four principles: We continue to accept that anxiety is natural but has become unhealthy (normalization). We then begin to better understand our fears and start facing them rather than avoiding them (exposure). We then use the new skills we are learning to become desensitized to our fears (habituation). In the process, we discover healthy ways to experience God's love for us and others (care).

The shower example illustrates desensitization through habituation. Habituation is the diminishing of a physiological or emotional response to a frequently repeated stimulus. By continually exposing ourselves to what makes us anxious (like me with the hot water), we become desensitized to the stimuli, and our anxiety diminishes over time. And it's important to keep in mind that our biology is doing a lot of the work here.

You've done this before. Just think of something you used to be afraid of that doesn't scare you anymore—swimming, speaking in public, animals. What did you do? You accepted the worry, faced your fear, dealt with the feelings, had others support you, and with repeated exposure, the anxiety decreased . . . and some of you even became surfers, public speakers, and animal lovers!

Our natural tendency is to avoid what makes us anxious, but we've learned that anxiety grows through avoidance. It seems counterintuitive because our instinct is to move away from things we fear. But for those of us with chronic worry, intrusive thoughts, and unwanted feelings, our fear is false. Our brains have learned to fear things we shouldn't fear.

A few years back I was on the phone with a mentor of mine. "I need to have a difficult conversation with a friend at work," I told him.

"How long have you been needing to talk to this person?" he asked.

"For about a month. I've been kind of avoiding it because I don't want to hurt her feelings."

He paused and then said, "You're not protecting her feelings; you're protecting your own. Is this person at work with you today?"

"Yes," I admitted.

"You need to share your observations with her. Share your desire to not hurt her and then be simple and direct. Hang up the phone now, go have a conversation with her, and then call me back."

Click.

Gulp.

I paced around my office and then decided to just do what he said. The conversation was very uncomfortable for me. But I found I was able to articulate myself better than I'd expected. I was able to be compassionate and candid. My friend was thankful to hear what I had to share and asked helpful questions. That's an example of exposure.

Some of you are freaking out right now. You're feeling what's called *anticipatory anxiety.*

But the more we face our fears, the easier it gets. It can be scary, but it works! What scares me the most is something called *flooding.* It's when we allow ourselves to have the intense emotions of anxiety. I find it helpful to simply acknowledge this in the moment by saying, "I'm feeling flooded right now. I can live with this feeling."

Even imagining a fear exposure—and feeling the anxiety of it— leverages the power of habituation. This is called *cognitive flooding.* For example, I have a close friend who has a lot of anxiety about talking to people in positions of authority. He's had some very negative experiences with employers in the past. He wants to overcome this fear. Sometimes, I will ask him to imagine a conversation with someone in authority and tell me how he feels. We'll stick with the imagined situation for as long as he can handle the feelings (and then usually a bit longer). It's a way for him to get used to the "hot water" of his feelings.

Exposure leads to habituation. Right!

Habituation leads to the realization that your most feared consequences won't happen. Wrong!

The goal of all of this is not to get rid of your fears. You *may* realize your worst fears won't come true, but if they do, you'll be able to see that it's not the end of the world. The main goal is to become more accepting of uncertainty and less reactive to your anxious thoughts and feelings.

If we are not regularly facing our fears, we'll stall in our spiritual growth. About a year ago, I took five weeks off from work. It was a tremendous gift. It was good for my mind, body, and spirit. Toward the end of that time, I went to see my counselor. He asked how I was doing with my anxiety. "I'm doing great!" I told him. "No panic attacks and no anxious moments. Is my anxiety gone?"

He listened graciously and then said, "No. You have no triggers. There's no exposure, so there's no growth. I'm glad it's been a season of rest. Let's get you ready to go back to normal life."

Seasons of rest and calm are wonderful. But we are learning practical skills to help us live in the real world and grow to be healthier. This involves facing the things that scare us.

ACTION STEPS

1. *Expose yourself to a fear.* Using your fear ladder, choose another fear to face. This could be a fear you've thought about facing before but decided not to do it. It could also be a fear you faced but could only tolerate for a short amount of time. Try enduring your anxious feelings a little longer this time. Consider using some of the spiritual exercises you've learned already, like gratefully reflecting on Psalm 139 or doing some spiritual reading. In the next section we'll explore some grounding exercises that will be helpful.

2. *Expect to feel worse before you feel better.* Habituation is exhausting. Exposure is exhausting. You are halfway through *The Anxiety Field Guide*, and you may be tired already. This is normal. Go back to the section on caring for your whole self. Make sure you are eating better, resting well, and finding some areas of spiritual encouragement. You might need to focus more on these areas as you continue.

3. *Celebrate past habituations.* Think of something that used to scare you but doesn't anymore (fear of the dark, rollercoasters, and so on). Why are you not scared anymore? Because you slowly and progressively faced your fears and retrained your brain. You've already practiced exposure and benefited from habituation in the past. Keep going!

18

Find Ways to Be Grounded

When caught in an anxious moment,
you can shift the way you are experiencing
the world. Healthy habits can help you
change direction and move forward.

IT WAS ONE OF THE MOST USUAL COUNSELING appointments of my life.

"I want you to think of a situation that brings you a lot of anxiety," my counselor told me.

"Got it," I said.

"What came to mind?"

"Not being far enough ahead of things at work."

"Okay," he said, "when I tell you, I want you to imagine yourself with a deadline approaching. Think of something specific. Something real. Allow all the anxious feelings to flood you. I'm going to ask you to experience your anxious feelings and do something else at the same time. We're going to do this exercise five different times. Ready?"

"Yes, I'm anxious. I mean, ready," I quipped.

He handed me a breath mint. He said, "While you are flooded with anxious feelings about that deadline, put this in your mouth and focus on the taste of it for thirty seconds." I did it, and after thirty seconds he asked, "What can you tell me about the taste?"

"It was cinnamon."

"How long could you focus on the taste before the anxious feelings took over again?"

"Just a few seconds."

He said, "Now, I want you to let yourself get flooded again with your anxious feelings about that deadline. Then look around the room for thirty seconds and notice as many things as possible. Go." After thirty seconds, he asked, "What did you notice around the office?"

"Not much. I was still thinking about the deadline."

Then he said, "Again, let yourself get flooded with your anxious feelings about that deadline. Then touch the fabric on your pant leg for thirty seconds." After thirty seconds he asked me what happened.

"The fabric was coarse. There were these little lines in it. That surprised me because I didn't think these pants had texture like that. And the lines had small bumps. As I rubbed my finger on them, they made me think about those bumps on the road that keep you in your lane."

"How long before the emotions of your deadline came back?"

I thought for a moment and said, "They just did."

His final two exercises involved listening for sounds in the room and smelling a candle. My response to listening for sounds was just like touching my pant leg: thirty seconds was not enough time! But after sniffing the candle, I was quickly returned to my anxious thoughts and feelings.

Then he said, "I'm going to share with you some research by a guy named Norman Farb. There are two ways the brain processes information. One way is through what's called your *narrative focus network*. When you're planning, strategizing, and ruminating, this is your narrative focus network at work. The other way your brain processes information is through what's called your *experiential focus network.* This is the way your brain processes being in the present moment. When you are experiencing your five senses, this is your experiential focus network.

"Now here's the important thing to know," he continued. "The narrative focus network and the experiential focus network can't operate at the same time. When you are caught in your anxious thoughts and feelings, that 'worry loop' is your narrative focus network on overdrive. You need to find ways to shift out of those loops to be more present in the moment in healthy ways, by engaging your experiential focus network."

Wow.

The narrative focus network is the default network of the human brain. It's wonderful. We take in information, process, plan, reason, forecast, analyze, and create stories to hold everything together. For those of us with anxiety, this is also where we confuse our feelings with facts, confirm our biases, condemn ourselves, and catastrophize.

The experiential focus network helps us encounter the world in real time. It helps us stop and smell the flowers, accept a compliment, appreciate the breath in our lungs, and be present with someone who is hurting without getting caught up in our need to fix them or take blame for their pain. It's one way we've been designed to experience God's loving presence in the present moment.

The simple exercise my therapist showed me helped me discover that when I'm caught up in the overwhelming flood of my anxiety, actively engaging my senses of touch and sound can create a dramatic shift in my brain and snap me out of my "worry loop."

In anxiety treatment, this is called *grounding.* Grounding is a way to help our brains change direction for a moment and think more healthily so we can more intentionally practice all the other skills and techniques we are learning.

God created us mind, body, and spirit. When we are anxious, we can use our God-given five senses to physiologically and spiritually remind ourselves that we are safe and secure in our Father's world. It's an invitation to grace, relationship with others, and rest from our anxious thoughts and feelings.

Let me stop here and make an important point about the goal of grounding. It is not intended to be a form of avoidance. When I first started dealing with my anxiety, I discovered that crafting was a hobby that helped me break out of my worry loops and find some peace. One day I found myself crafting for eight hours straight! I realized I was avoiding my anxiety by escaping into something healthy.

The purpose of grounding exercises is not to give you an escape from dealing with your anxiety. The purpose is to help shift your focus so you can practice normalization, exposure, habituation, and care. Grounding helps us dig our feet into the ground to face our fears, not run from them.

ACTION STEPS

1. *Discover which of your five senses grounds you.* Do the grounding exercise for yourself. Ask someone to help you if that's easier. Think of something that brings you anxiety. Imagine it in order to produce your anxious thoughts and feelings (that is, cognitive flooding). Engage one of your senses. Repeat this for each of your senses. Determine which of your senses are most helpful in grounding you when you are flooded with anxiety.

2. *Plan for "mobile grounding."* We cannot control when we feel anxious, so we need grounding exercises wherever we go. Plan how you can use a simple grounding technique wherever you are. For example, if taste helps change mental direction during an anxious moment, carry breath mints on you. If it's touch, you could plan to rub your fingers together. Remember, grounding is a simple trick to empower us to use other skills. If you use it to avoid, it can become a compulsion or a tick.

3. *Find hobbies that ground you.* God has given you gifts and talents to help you stay grounded when anxiety hits. Are you artistic? Be creative—draw or use coloring books, create or appreciate music, write, dance, act, build crafts. Are you athletic? Be active—run, lift, hike, or practice yoga or martial arts. Are you a tactile person? Engage with the natural world—garden, cook, take photos, hike, do woodworking. Develop ongoing ways of nurturing your God-given senses. This will help you with your anxiety. Also, helping children find healthy habits and hobbies when they are young can prepare them to deal with anxiety better as they age.

19

Be Courageously Vulnerable

You have learned to self-protect, hide,
and defend yourself. You can begin to admit
your struggles and share with others.

Y EARS AGO, I RAN OVER a cat with my car. It wasn't on purpose. I was driving home late one night and heard a thud. I pulled over to see what had happened. A black and gray cat was lying motionless on the street. I felt so guilty.

I didn't want it to get hit by another car, so I decided to move it out of the middle of the street. As I approached it, it started to move around. It tried to stand up, but its hind legs weren't cooperating. I was so happy it was alive but so sad it was injured.

As I got close enough to help, it turned to me and hissed! I jumped back in fear. Then I yelled at it, "I'm trying to help you!" It started to drag itself away from me while continuing to hiss.

That cat did what all of God's creatures are designed to do when vulnerable—self-protect.

It's a survival technique to avoid further harm. When we feel weak, insecure, lonely, scared, and defenseless, our instinct is to attack, run, or play dead. This self-protection response isn't just instinctual, it's also learned. Before we're even able to articulate our thoughts and feelings, we learn how to make self-protecting decisions when we feel unsafe.

After our daughter Elia was born, my wife, Marie, suffered a terrible season of postpartum depression. For the first couple of years of my daughter's life, Marie was not available to her emotionally, and sometimes physically. By the age of three, Elia struggled with closeness with others. She had huge emotional outbursts and didn't want to be held or hugged by anyone. When people wanted to be close to her, she'd act out by withdrawing.

Our family got professional help, and Marie and Elia are both in great places emotionally and relationally these days. Elia doesn't remember that difficult stage of her life, but Marie and I call that time "the feral years." The word *feral* refers to a domesticated animal that has learned to survive on its own. Without care, nurture, training, and love, animals resort to radical self-protection.

We do that too.

The opposite of radical self-protection is courageous vulnerability. Instead of attacking, running, or playing dead when we feel weak, insecure, lonely, scared, and defenseless, we can reach out for help. We can be aware of our thoughts and feelings, learn to articulate them, and ask for what we need. We can also develop the emotional resilience to handle life when we don't get what we ask for. That's what it means to be vulnerable and courageous.

Courage is not the absence of fear. Courage is pushing through fear. Our survival instinct will tell us, "Protect what you have, and don't ask for what you need." But courage says, "It may be scary, but be honest and risk going after what you need."

Some of us are not courageously vulnerable because we have reached out for help in the past and it wasn't there. Anxiety keeps us feral. Here's what that could look like.

When we're feeling anxious, we hiss at others who want to help. We may have learned that when we're vulnerable, we get hurt. This has made us overprotective of ourselves. Being courageously vulnerable means reaching out to others for help. It may take time to find the right helpful relationships, but each attempt is worth it. We can say, "I'm going to try again."

When we're feeling anxious, we avoid what scares us. We think we are protecting ourselves by isolating, but we need to share our fears with others. Facing uncertainty is what we have in common with all human beings. Being courageously vulnerable means sharing our struggles with uncertainty with people. We can say, "There are others like me."

When we're feeling anxious, we feel shame. We're embarrassed by our worry, fear, and intrusive thoughts or feelings. Rather than fixing or following our fears, we can unshame our worry by opening up to those we trust. Courageous vulnerability can help us express our insecurities. We can say, "I'm feeling kind of tender right now."

In a previous section, I referred to Jesus praying on the night before he was crucified. Knowing he would be arrested and die, he went to an isolated area and asked his closest friends to come with him. After agonizing in prayer, he found that his friends had fallen asleep! He said, "Couldn't you watch with me even one hour?" (Matthew 26:40). He was disappointed and expressed it. If Jesus reached out to others at his most vulnerable times, maybe we can too!

Vulnerability is about being exposed to the possibility of being hurt or disappointed. We should not be vulnerable with people we know will intentionally victimize us. Some of us have learned to subject ourselves to physical, sexual, emotional, verbal, and spiritual abuse. That's not courageous vulnerability. It's called *learned helplessness*, and it's something we can get help to unlearn.

Courageous vulnerability is learning to move from a pattern of self-protection to being more open with people who care about us. This doesn't mean we will never experience problems in our relationships. Courageous vulnerability is about pushing past the unhealthy fears that are keeping us from being known and loved by others.

The first time I shared my anxiety with the people at my church was during a Sunday service. There were hundreds of people present. I knew sharing my story was another part of exposure. I told myself that some people would not understand what I was talking about. They would want to fix me or even judge me (and some did). But I also told myself there would be many others who would be grateful that I was courageously vulnerable, and my courageous words would make some of them feel less alone. And that's exactly what happened.

ACTION STEPS

1. *Share what you're learning with someone new.* By now, I hope you have one or two close companions you trust. They've been hearing about your journey and may be helping you with some of the action steps. Now, reach out to share your experiences with someone new. Maybe bring it up casually and mention that you're reading this book. You don't have to give your life story. In fact, don't. Just share a little about your anxiety. This will continue to help reduce the shame. If you haven't found one or two close companions yet, this can help you get started. Some people find support groups to be safe places to experiment in reducing shame. Look for a support group in your area.

2. *Use more "I" statements when communicating.* Own your thoughts and feelings by saying "I" instead of "you," especially when it comes to expressing your hurts and disappointments. For example, instead of saying, "You hurt me," try saying, "I feel hurt." Instead of saying, "You rejected me," try saying, "I feel lonely." This will help you take responsibility for your feelings. You may also want to work on increasing your "feeling vocabulary" to better communicate your feelings. For example, instead of saying "sad," try being more specific, like depressed, guilty, bored, tired, ashamed, or lonely. I've included a feelings wheel at the end of this chapter to help.

3. *Ask God to continue to help you with courageous vulnerability.* The apostle Paul wrote these words to his young protégé Timothy: "For God has not given us a spirit of fear and timidity, but of power, love, and self-discipline" (2 Timothy 1:7). We have learned over time to be fearful and timid, but God is helping us develop new spiritual disciplines so we can live in his power and love. Thank God for the progress you have made, and continue to lean on his love and power.

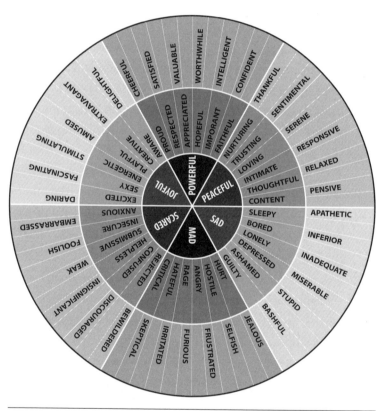

Figure 19.1. Feelings wheel

20

Prepare for Exposure Fatigue

Changing how you deal with your anxiety is exhausting. Plan to care for yourself after long struggles with your unwanted thoughts and feelings.

IT WAS ANOTHER SLEEPLESS NIGHT of worrying. I tried to shut off the thoughts, distracted myself, practiced some mindfulness techniques, prayed, read the same paragraphs of a book over and over, and paced through the house for hours. Unable to shake my anxious thoughts and feelings, I watched the sun rise. I felt defeated.

I told my counselor about it at my next appointment. "Nothing worked," I said. "I tried to not have anxiety and it was still there. I did all the things I know. I was a mess the next day."

"What did you do the next day?" my counselor asked.

"I went into work, but I didn't get anything done. I was so exhausted. I felt defeated—again."

"Could you have taken a sick day?"

"I guess. But I'm not sick. It was my fault. I stayed up all night."

He paused and then said gently, "You have anxiety. That's like a sickness, and maybe you could make some room for that as you are getting well."

For some of us, anxiety is like a sickness that's strongest at night.

Someone once said, "Lights out, anxiety on." The quietness of the night acts as an invitation to overthinking, and when our body is on high alert, falling asleep is the most unnatural expectation. That's why insomnia is a common side effect of anxiety. Here are a few unique characteristics of late-night anxiety battles.

Loneliness. The night feels lonelier than the day. This could be because our body's circadian rhythm is telling us that this is when we should be sleeping. The quietness can be deafening.

When we turn on a TV (or computer) or listen to music, the night has a loudness of its own.

If we live with others, we can see and hear their peaceful rest. They are enjoying sleep along with millions of others around the world. This makes us feel more alone—and jealous.

Anger. Inability to sleep awakens a unique form of self-anger. Sleep is one of the several body responses that you can't make happen. It has to happen to you. It's an act of grace. I believe this is why insomnia easily angers us. It's a reminder that we are not in control. The more you try to go to sleep, the more it fights back. It's a bit like trying to stop our anxiety! When we do finally fall asleep (if we do), our last interaction with ourselves is anger.

Anticipation anxiety. When we're up all night, we aren't just worried about how to get to sleep. We're also worried about how our lack of sleep will affect us the next day. We have responsibilities. We know we will not be rested or in the right frame of mind. This creates more anxiety. There's a special file of self-condemning messages in our mind that automatically opens at night. When we have insomnia, we say the worst things to ourselves.

Here's the good news: we can prepare for nighttime battles with anxiety and the days that follow.

Your "anxiety all-nighters" are times to practice habituation. Rather than try to force yourself to sleep, act on compulsions, or give into unhealthy behaviors to soothe yourself, use the time to apply the new skills you are learning.

You'll probably be drained mentally, emotionally, and physically, but as you continue to apply your new skills and practices, these all-nighters will become less frequent. When they do happen, be prepared for what happens next: exposure fatigue.

In the past, when we'd worry, we'd act on our compulsions or do something to numb ourselves. Now, we are exposing our brain and body to something new—now we're trying to endure our anxious thoughts and feelings without trying to fight, run from, or be paralyzed by inaction. And it can be draining.

Have you ever been exhausted after a good workout? When you exercise, you're taking your body and mind past the comfort zone. The next day you may feel tired and achy. When this happens, you don't say, "Wow, I should never do that again." Instead, you recover by caring for yourself, and then you work out again. Exposure and habituation are like working out; we keep doing simple, strategic exercises, and it can be exhausting at first.

But what about the next day?

After an anxiety all-nighter, you won't be in top form. You'll be moody, restless, and probably feeling guilty about your inability to just "fix" your anxiety. Try looking at it as having been sick the night before or having done a huge workout. What do you do on those days?

Sometimes you can't change anything. The homework is due, the interview is happening, the sale needs to be finalized. You have to just do the best you can. You may have to accept that you'll be less productive and less relational, and you will need to modify your expectations of yourself.

You can also let people know what you're feeling. When this happens to me, I'll say to the people closest to me, "I had a tough night with anxiety last night, so thanks for being gracious with me." To those less close to me, I say, "I'm feeling a little under the weather today. Nothing contagious, but I'm not playing my A-game today. Thanks for understanding."

If possible, you could take a sick day. This could mean taking a day off or just changing your schedule by going in late, leaving early, or moving some appointments to another day. This isn't a way to avoid anxiety but a way of creating space to work on your anxiety. It's only for a season. Through continued habituation and caring for your whole self, the anxiety will diminish and your exposure fatigue will lessen.

ACTION STEPS

1. *Prepare for anxiety all-nighters.* We can't schedule our insomnia, but we can accept it as a normal side effect of anxiety. Instead of being surprised and frustrated when it happens, we can use it to move us forward on the path of freedom. What healthy habits and practices can you have available for all-nighters? These "just in case I'm up" activities could include home projects, crafting, movie watching, and letter writing.

2. *Give yourself grace with exposure fatigue.* Your anxiety-inspired insomnia is not a sign of failure. It's a symptom of a problem you're working on. Go easy on yourself the next day. Celebrate whatever skills, new spiritual disciplines, and practices you tried during the night. Being angry, disappointed, or intolerant only aggravates your anxiety, so speak kindly to yourself and remember that you are working on a plan to get better. It will take some time, but you're making progress.

21

Choose Joy

Anxiety grows when you feed it.
You can make positive choices to focus
on what brings you joy and limit your time
focusing on what triggers your anxiety.

MY DAUGHTER WAS GOING THROUGH the refrigerator and found something in the back that had gone bad. "Ewww," she said, "this smells horrible! Here, smell it!"

"I don't want to smell it!" I told her. "If it went bad, get rid of it. I don't need to smell it!"

Why do people do that? They smell something terrible, and they want us to smell it too! A lot of things in my world stink; I don't need you to put something else under my nose.

I believe the dramatic upswing in anxiety among young people is due in part to them being bombarded with information, statistics, news, updates, and warnings from around the world of things to be worried about. This ends up being a form of "vicarious trauma" as we're exposed to more suffering than we're designed to handle.

We live in an anxiety-feeding culture. Fear, worry, and bad news sell, and we are always buying. But we have a choice. We can take back our lives by choosing what gets our focus. We can choose joy.

Here's some powerful advice on anxiety from the apostle Paul:

Always be full of joy in the Lord. I say it again—rejoice! Let
everyone see that you are considerate in all you do. Remember,
the Lord is coming soon.

Don't worry about anything; instead, pray about everything.
Tell God what you need, and thank him for all he has done.
Then you will experience God's peace, which exceeds anything
we can understand. His peace will guard your hearts and minds
as you live in Christ Jesus. (Philippians 4:4-7)

My first thought after reading this was, *That's easy for you to say!
You have no idea what I'm going through.* But the more I learn about
Paul, the more I realize maybe he was onto something! He followed
Jesus into some of the most stressful, fearful, and anxiety-inducing
situations we can imagine.

Paul wrote these words from prison. He had been arrested for starting churches in areas where talking about Jesus was illegal. He had
been beaten up and threatened, struggled with poverty and physical illness, and was on a ship that crashed. He knew what anxiety was about.
From these difficulties, he gives some challenging spiritual advice. He
starts off by saying "rejoice" and then gives us some ways to do that.

First, he reminds us to be considerate of others. When we are
anxious, we often spill that stress onto other people. One way to
experience joy is to find ways to positively impact other people. One
way I've done this is by writing notes of gratitude. When I am feeling
anxious, I will think of people who have really helped me over the
years and let them know how I am thankful for them. A small act of
gratitude can starve anxiety and make room for joy.

Second, he recommends prayer. Simply tell God what you need.
Sometimes we make prayer another way to ruminate on our worries.
Simple, brief requests can help us focus on how God loves us, knows
us, and wants to help us. Anticipating God's help—in whatever form
that may take—can increase our joy. But remember, prayer is more

than just asking God for help. It's remembering his promises and thanking him for the many things we have already received from him. Prayer is an invitation to realign our thoughts and feelings away from what makes us anxious and back with God's plan, purpose, and promises.

Third, he says that we can experience God's peace in a way we might not understand. I think there have been a few times when I have experienced this kind of peace he's describing. I found myself saying, "I'd normally be really worried right now, but I'm not!" Those are sweet moments. I'd like to experience them more often. But what do we do when we still can't find peace?

I think the answer to this question is found in what Paul writes next: "Dear brothers and sisters, one final thing. Fix your thoughts on what is true, and honorable, and right, and pure, and lovely, and admirable. Think about things that are excellent and worthy of praise" (Philippians 4:8).

He's saying to keep your focus on what God has done, is doing, and will do. The more we do this, the less time and energy we have for focusing on our fears. You might be asking, "Isn't that like putting our heads in the ground and ignoring the problems?" Nope. Focusing on the good is not ignoring the bad; it's putting the bad in its proper place.

He ends with this beautiful statement: "Whatever you have learned or received or heard from me, or seen in me—put it into practice. And the God of peace will be with you" (Philippians 4:9 NIV). He's saying, "Start practicing this and you'll see spiritual change in your life."

What you reinforce gets increased. This is the key to great parenting. For example, if you focus your attention on your child's bad behaviors, your child registers that as "parental attention" and will continue in the bad behavior for more attention. If you reward and reinforce the good behavior, your child will want to do good. The bad behavior is starved of attention.

The same is true of anxiety. Our anxious thoughts and feelings grow stronger from the attention we give them. We shouldn't ignore or avoid what brings us anxiety, but our fullest attention should be given to what brings joy to us and what brings joy to God!

I was reading a book by a sixteenth-century Catholic spiritual theologian named Francis de Sales. De Sales describes the terrible living conditions of cities near him. Congested populations and poor sanitation meant that walking through the cities stank—literally. The smell was awful. Unable to change the population density and waste management, people created their own way to deal with the smell. It was called a *nosegay*. They would gather a small collection of beautifully scented flowers and hold them under their nose as they went about their day. This allowed them a pleasant smell as they went about their business.

Francis de Sales suggests that we should all have a daily "spiritual nosegay"—a collection of positive thoughts, spiritual quotes, or promises from God that can help us get through the stink and smell of this world. A spiritual nosegay can help us stay focused on the positive while fighting injustice, oppression, and selfishness around us as well as the anxiety within us.

ACTION STEPS

1. *Carry something positive into your day.* Create a way to start your day with joy. This could be a quiet time of reflection, prayer, and gratitude. It could be reminding yourself of something good from the previous day or week. Don't make it lengthy or complicated. The goal is to start the day with joyful reflection to carry with you. Consider doing something similar before bedtime to finish the day with joy, reflecting on the good you found during the day.

2. *Veer toward the positive.* Identify those areas that cause you to "veer toward the stink." Is it gossip, criticism, rumors, inhospitality, clickbait, or other people's drama? When you experience these things, resist letting them awaken your anxiety.

Instead, find positive ways to respond, or leave the situation and find something more enjoyable that deserves your attention. You may want to let those closest to you know that you are experimenting with this.

3. *Look for opportunities to laugh.* Joy and happiness are not the same thing, but they both share one thing in common: laughter. Laughter is good for the body and soul. It decreases stress hormones, boosts the immune system, releases endorphins, burns calories, and increases blood flow. It also lightens the heavy load of our souls. You are doing a lot of important work with your anxiety. You deserve to laugh. Find things that make you laugh!

22

Examine Your Core Beliefs and Distortions

Your anxiety is directly shaped
by very common errors in thinking.
Changing your thinking habits can have
a positive impact on the rest of your life.

THE HOUSE I GREW UP IN was always shifting. It was built on a tough adobe soil, and if the soil wasn't watered regularly and properly, it would crack, and the house would "settle." It didn't help that we lived in California where we also had earthquakes! Sometimes when I was bored, I'd lie on my back in the living room and count the cracks in our ceiling.

We could always tell if the house had shifted because the front door would stick. We'd have to pull up or down on the door handle to get it to lock. Sometimes we'd have to drill a larger hole (higher or lower) so the deadbolt would lock.

Our home was literally full of cracks and always shifting, but I got used to it. Over time, I didn't even notice it. Eventually, we had a structural engineer go under the house, examine the foundation, and give us advice on how to prevent future damage.

The house I grew up in is a good metaphor for what goes on in our minds. From our very early years, we begin to form a set of core beliefs or values that become the foundation for our lives. Some of our core beliefs were explicitly taught to us by parents, caregivers, peers, and authority figures. We learned other core beliefs by cause and effect—watching other people's examples or just figuring out what we needed to do to survive.

These core beliefs answer questions like, Who am I? How does the world work? Who can I trust? What is my purpose in life? The answers to these questions powerfully shape our thinking and actions. And like the foundation of a home, most of the answers to these questions are not easily visible. They reside deep within us, and we usually only become aware of them in times of change, stress, and loss.

Anxiety can make us more aware of our core beliefs. Anxiety also can help us see that some of our core beliefs, like the foundation of a home, are no longer able to uphold the weight of our life and circumstances. We may have core beliefs about how we view ourselves, others, the world, or God that are not true. We may also have very common ways of thinking that lead us to unhealthy conclusions. These are called *cognitive distortions*.

Cognitive distortions are biased ways of thinking that reinforce false beliefs about yourself and the world around you. They developed when you were young, changed over time, and like your personality, they are basically part of a larger "survival strategy" you've developed to make sense of your life. But by now, they're doing you more harm than good.

We all have cognitive distortions. Here are some examples.

Black and white thinking. This is an "all or nothing" way of seeing things. You group things into binary categories—great or horrible, right or wrong, innocent or guilty. You also exaggerate things so they'll fit into these either-or categories. Rather than thinking in simple categories, you can begin to see things on a continuum.

Inflated sense of responsibility. You believe that you have more control than you do. You take responsibility for other people's thoughts, feelings, and actions. When something goes wrong, you say, "That was all my fault," or, "I should have done something to prevent that." Rather than owning other people's responsibilities, you can empower others to take responsibility for themselves.

Name-calling and labeling. You say things about yourself that are not true, are overly critical of yourself, and attribute false motives to your thoughts and feelings. You call yourself "dumb" or "ugly" or "lazy." You may even convince yourself that your name-calling is helpful. Rather than condemning yourself, you can discover ways to see and celebrate your strengths.

Mind reading. You assume you know what people are thinking or feeling. You confuse your feelings with theirs. You attribute motives to people that aren't accurate. You may also believe that if people cared about you more, they'd know your thoughts and feelings. Rather than mind reading, you can learn to ask questions of others and share what's happening with you.

Dismissing the positive. You have a mental filter that emphasizes the negative over the positive. This comes from your overactive threat center wanting to be prepared for any problem. This may also be a habit you've formed because you felt unsafe and unready for life's challenges. Rather than always seeing the negative, you can intentionally nurture hope, faith, and love.

Emotional reasoning. You confuse feelings with facts. You believe if you feel it, it must be true. You learned to think with your emotions rather than feel with them. Rather than believing what you feel, you can learn to live with the tension of listening to your emotions while judging reality on rational evidence.

Catastrophizing. You jump to conclusions, imagine worst-case scenarios, and believe one negative event represents a bigger pattern of defeat. You predict and overprepare for bad things that will likely never happen. Rather than focusing on what could happen, you can start focusing on the good that is happening, which can prepare you for the future.

Here's a story of how I experienced all these cognitive distortions in one moment. About two years into my role as lead pastor at our church, we entered a season of change management. Our church is over a hundred years old. We never change our message, but we are always changing our methods. Knowing that change is difficult for people, I remember saying to myself, "This is going to be awful (black and white thinking). I'm going to hurt people (inflated sense of responsibility) because I'm incompetent (name-calling/labeling). People are going to hate this (mind reading). This is all bad (dismissing the positive)—I can feel it (emotional reasoning). They may end up firing me (catastrophizing)."

It ended up being a challenging season at our church, but many wonderful, amazing, and life-giving things came from it. There were losses and difficult conversations, but with all the changes, there were great opportunities for new beginnings, relationships, and growth. The same is true when making changes in how we think about ourselves, others, the world, and God.

ACTION STEPS

1. *Make a list of your core beliefs.* Ask yourself these questions: What are my core beliefs about myself, people, the world, and God? Where did I get these beliefs? Is the source of these beliefs reliable? How have these beliefs changed over time? Have these beliefs changed for the better, or have my beliefs become more negative, cynical, or biased because of my anxiety? How can I find more clarity and hope in my beliefs?

2. *Identify your cognitive distortions.* Which of the cognitive distortions in this section resonate most with you? What are some examples of how these distortions play out in your life? How can you more quickly identify your cognitive distortions when

you talk, write, and pray? Who can you invite into this awareness to help you change your cognitive distortions?

3. *Explore Jesus' teachings as a foundation for your core beliefs.* In a famous collection of Jesus' teachings known as the Sermon on the Mount (Matthew 5–7), he speaks about life, spiritual habits, possessions, relationships, generosity, criticism, discernment, and worry. At the end, he compares these teachings to a house built on a secure foundation. Read through Matthew 5–7. Consider how what Jesus teaches can confirm some of your core beliefs and challenge some of your cognitive distortions.

23

Decouple Your Thoughts and Actions

Just because you thought it
or felt it doesn't mean you did it or will do it.
Resist unnecessary guilt and shame
by decoupling your thoughts and actions.

I **WAS TALKING TO A FRIEND** about a dream I'd had the night before. "It was the 1920s," I said, "and I was a bank robber. I was wearing this pinstripe suit. The bank was fancy with high ceilings. I yelled at people to stay on the floor, and my voice echoed throughout the place. There were three of us. We robbed the place and took the money out in bags. As I ran out of the bank, a security guard shot at me. I had this Tommy gun. So I just started shooting back. As the bullets were going into the guy, somehow I knew he had three daughters and they'd never see their daddy again. Then I woke up."

"Wow," he said. "I wish I had dreams like that!"

"You do?" I said, surprised. "I woke up feeling all shaky and kind of bad."

"What do you mean, bad?" he asked.

"I was a criminal and I killed people."

"Yeah, but it was just a dream. You didn't really do it."

"I know," I said, "but it felt like I did."

I don't have any desire to rob a bank or shoot someone on the way to my getaway car. I didn't choose to dream about being a violent criminal. Yet these unwanted thoughts during my sleep still created feelings of guilt and responsibility. I felt like I had really committed the act.

This is an illustration of a common experience among people with obsessive-compulsive disorder. It's called *thought-action fusion.*

Thought-action fusion is when we believe that just having a thought is equivalent to carrying out the action. For example, have you ever had a random thought of someone dying and then felt guilty for having had that thought? This is thought-action fusion. It's also when we believe that thinking something makes it more likely to happen. Have you ever had a random, unwanted thought of your plane crashing and then felt fearful of going on the plane?

Thought-action fusion is like the idea of "jinxing" something by saying it. It's rooted in the false belief that our thoughts are more important than they are. We may believe that our thoughts are dangerous in and of themselves or that they represent our true selves and could lead to dangerous actions. This cognitive error can feed our anxiety.

It doesn't help that our culture feeds this cognitive error. Pop psychologists, motivational gurus, and urban mystics teach that all our thoughts and feelings spring up from and represent our true selves and hold potential insight into past lives, nuggets of evolutionary wisdom, or soulish premonitions to be honored. We are even taught that we can create our own reality by believing things into existence.

Religious teaching may complicate this for us. Christianity offers a complex picture of the human condition, including the idea that we all possess an evil impulse, sinful nature, or "fleshly" part of ourselves that drives us to resist God's loving plan for our lives. But some people emphasize this so much that it drowns out the life-giving truth that we are all made in God's image and God wants to work in and through us for good. Our anxiety can lead us to believe that we are unlovable sinners and without hope before a holy God.

We all have random, unwanted thoughts and feelings. By no choice of our own, all kinds of unusual, taboo, and even disturbing things can pop into our minds. When this happens, thought-action fusion may cause us to hear these internal messages:

How could you even think that?

No one has feelings like that!

Only someone like you could imagine such a terrible thing!

Shame on you for having that thought!

Can our thoughts be bad or evil? Yes. Jesus warned that we should be careful not to give in to our bad or evil thoughts or feelings (Matthew 5:22, 28). But those of us with anxiety sometimes confuse having an unwanted thought or feeling with a sinful action. When we mistake a thought or feeling with an action, we feel misplaced guilt or shame, our anxiety spikes, and we may want to soothe ourselves. We might feel the sudden urge to practice a ritual to calm ourselves. The problem is, we didn't do anything wrong! We just had an unwanted thought or feeling.

Just because you think it or feel it doesn't mean you'll do it.

At least four times in my life, I have had the thought of taking my own life. I won't give you the specific details of those times, but they were quite intense. I never once actually tried to end my life. I didn't want to do it! In fact, the idea of doing it really bothered me. I became kind of obsessed with my fear of these thoughts. This is sometimes called *suicidal OCD*.

The main difference between intrusive thoughts of suicide and actual suicidal thinking is intention. Unlike someone with actual suicidal thinking, those of us with intrusive thoughts don't want to die by suicide and obsess about how to make sure we don't. We fear that thinking about it will cause it to happen.

Let me stop here and say, if you have thoughts of self-harm or suicide, don't try to figure them out on your own. Reach out to a professional or call a suicide hotline to speak with someone. One thing that both intrusive thoughts of suicide and actual suicidal thinking have in common is that we need help from others with both.

The good news is the thought-action fusion can be addressed by something called *decoupling*. Decoupling is the mental act of unfusing our intrusive thoughts and feelings from the unhealthy messages that accompany them. It involves actively testing the link between your thoughts and actions to provide yourself evidence to challenge your feelings. For example, if you are afraid something bad will happen to you if you go outside, go outside. This will be anxiety producing, but it will help you decouple your fears about what could happen. Of course, this does not provide absolute certainty that bad things will not happen. The uncertainty that remains is what you must learn to tolerate.

ACTION STEPS

1. *Practice decoupling.* Identify an intrusive thought or feeling that you fear may lead to something bad. Spend time imagining it happening. After doing this, engage in a positive activity or action of your choice—go for a walk, write an encouraging note to someone, or listen to some music you enjoy. Allow yourself to realize that your thought was not dangerous and did not lead to harm.

2. *Talk with someone you trust about an unverbalized fear.* Fear grows in the darkness. Bring it into the light. Share an intrusive thought or feeling with someone you trust. Explain why you're afraid it will lead to something dangerous. Oftentimes, explaining it out loud to someone helps us hear the flaws in our logic. This can help us doubt the messages associated with our fears.

24

Look for the Umbrella

*Many things have helped you feel protected
from the storms of life. The loss of any of them
may hold the key to your struggles with anxiety.*

I HAVE A FRIEND who used to carry an umbrella everywhere. If it wasn't in his hand, it was in his car or office. He said it was just in case it rained—but we lived in an area of Southern California where it rarely rains.

I always thought he was overprepared—until it rained. Then he'd say, "See? I knew I would need this." What was great is that he always had an umbrella and was prepared for the rain. What wasn't great was how obsessed he was with having an umbrella with him all the time.

Why didn't he just check the weather and use an umbrella when he needed it? I don't believe the umbrella was to protect him from rain. It was protecting him from his anxiety about the unknown. The umbrella was a powerful reminder that he was safe and that in the event of something bad, he'd be okay.

We all have our umbrellas.

Here are different kinds of umbrellas that give us a sense of safety.

Our core beliefs. Most of us operate from a set of unverbalized core beliefs. They can be beliefs about how the world works, like, "If I am a good person, bad things won't happen to me," or, "God won't give me more than I can handle." They can be beliefs about relationships, like, "I will never get divorced," or, "I'm going to find the perfect soulmate one day." These beliefs can be about other things too, like "I'll have this job until I retire," or, "If I take care of myself, I won't get sick." Our core beliefs give us a sense of safety from the fearful things of the world.

Our core relationships. Some key relationships are our family of origin, friendships, romantic relationships, and spiritual mentors or companions. All these relationships, functional and dysfunctional, symbolically help us navigate the unknown. Without ever verbalizing their support, they often remind us that while everything around us can change, we are loved, known, and accepted. We may not even be consciously aware of how important they are to our sense of security until they're gone.

Our connection to God. We all have beliefs about what role God plays in our lives. We have beliefs about God's presence, how much God determines to happen, and where our free will comes in. We also have beliefs about God's love for us and protection of us. We have strong, often unverbalized beliefs about how God responds to us when we make mistakes or sin. Some of us have a healthy balance of God's holiness and love, while others of us veer toward one of these more than the other. We also have beliefs about how much we can trust other Jesus-followers in our lives.

What happens when you lose your umbrella?

I was eleven years old when my dad died. He struggled for two years with leukemia which, at the time, was explained to me as "blood cancer." I saw him grow thinner and thinner, endure full-body chemotherapy and a bone marrow transplant, and then get double pneumonia. The last time I saw him, he was on a ventilator. He used a board with letters on it to spell out the words I AM PROUD OF YOU.

My dad was a strong and silent man. He was both technical and artistic. He had a quick wit. From school, Little League, and Cub Scouts to hanging out in the garage while he made things out of wood, the world made a little more sense with my dad in it. I always felt like he was there for me.

My dad died just as I was entering puberty—just when I started needing him in a new way. His death changed our family forever. I remember the arguments and the emotional distance, and how we all started finding our new roles in the family. Mine was the peacemaker and comforter. Added to all this, it was the eighties. My older brother and I were classic Gen Xers (before that generation even had a name). Mom went to work and we were "latchkey kids," on our own from three to six in the afternoon, watching TV and playing video games.

My mom was amazing. She taught me how to grieve. But my dad was an umbrella. Without him (and with the terrible nature of his illness and death), the world seemed less safe and less predictable. I couldn't articulate it at the time, but I felt vulnerable. I didn't know what to do with those vulnerable feelings.

Have you lost an umbrella?

The death of a loved one, a traumatic event, health issues, the loss of a child, divorce, financial loss, abuse, or a sense of disconnection from God can be the starting point for struggles with anxiety. It can be something big or something small that was big to you. Maybe it's something that created a sense of vulnerability in you.

Not all anxiety is born out of a trauma or an ungrieved loss. In fact, it's easy for those of us with anxiety to get overfixated on the origins of our anxiety when that might not really be important at all. What's important is that anxiety can be fueled by our feelings of vulnerability and loss of control. Sometimes these feelings began at a specific point in our past.

We all have umbrellas. They can be our beliefs, our relationships, or the ways we make sense of the unknown. The loss of any of those can hold the key to our struggles with anxiety. Exploring our ungrieved losses, traumas, and difficult seasons of the past can help us face our vulnerabilities in a new way and give us strength to face our anxious thoughts and feelings.

ACTION STEPS

1. *Create a life map.* Draw a line that represents your lifetime from birth to the present day. Then divide that line into different segments of your life. These segments could be years, school ages, or significant events. Record high points above the line and low points below the line at the times of life they occurred. Rank them in intensity by placing them higher or lower from your line. Write what the events were and what effect they had on your thoughts and feelings. Connect all the points with another line. I've included my life map at the end of this chapter as a sample.

2. *Identify your high and low points that could use more attention.* On your life map, which high points have you not truly celebrated? How could you remember, enjoy, and memorialize them more? Which low points have you ignored, minimized, or not fully grieved? Sometimes, we are moving so quickly that we don't fully grieve losses and traumas in our lives. For me, two of the events "below the line" became the focus of some important counseling and prayer times. Also, who were the people who most helped you during those high and low points? I included their names on my life map. After I finished it, I wrote them personal notes to thank them for the role they played during those times.

3. *Partner with a professional.* If you are not already seeing a counselor to help you, I highly recommend it. It's not a sign of weakness, it's a sign of strength! It takes courage to say, "I need some help here." A skilled counselor to help with anxiety will do a combination of cognitive-behavioral therapy (CBT) and exposure and response prevention (ERP). There are also some other ways they can help, like eye movement desensitization and reprocessing (EMDR) and medications if needed.

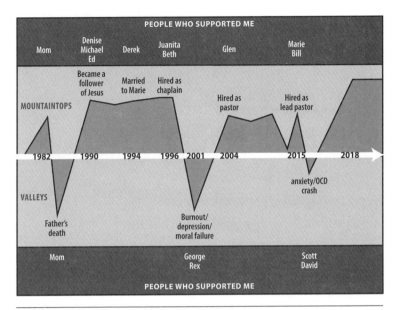

Figure 24.1. Life map

25

Reduce Your Self-Medicating

You've developed ways to soothe your anxious self.
As you learn new skills for dealing with anxiety,
you can reduce the unhealthy ways you self-medicate.

G ROWING UP WITHOUT A FATHER was tough. I often felt lonely and insecure. I couldn't put words to these feelings at that age, but I wanted to escape these feelings, even if only for a little while. Certain things made me feel better. Playing with my friends, watching movies, and drawing were some of the healthy activities that helped me feel happier. But when I was twelve years old, I discovered pornography in my friend's garage.

When I saw those explicit images, something happened in me. Those images fueled some powerful chemicals in my brain in a way I hadn't expected. For a moment, my anxious thoughts were quieted, and my unwanted feelings were soothed. I didn't know it at the time, but that day I discovered something to self-medicate my anxiety. I just didn't realize it would complicate it as well.

We anxious people make these discoveries. Usually unintentionally, we find activities that provide us temporary relief from our chronic worry, intrusive thoughts, and unwanted feelings.

Healthy discoveries include some of the healthy habits we've been exploring—identifying our anxiety for what it is, engaging and not avoiding, doubting the truthfulness of our feelings, developing healthy habits, positive self-talk, practicing mindfulness, and working with a professional counselor.

We also discover unhealthy ways of dealing with our anxiety—ways to turn off, suspend, or get rid of those bad feelings for a time. They become like a medicine we can give ourselves, but we don't realize the side effects that appear later.

Here are some common ways you may self-medicate your anxiety.

Distraction. You overindulge in television, video games, exercise, or other normal activities, but you do them as a form of avoidance. I love watching movies. While there's nothing inherently wrong with this, I believe my love for movies stemmed from my loneliness growing up. Unable to share my deep feelings, I poured myself into films as a form of self-medicating.

Relationships. You depend on others to change your mood, try to get others worried about your worries, are overly critical or impatient, or avoid relationships altogether. Some of my self-medicating through relationships involves being indirect and evasive because I'm afraid of disappointing people. I am learning to love people by being honest with them and myself.

Controlling. You overschedule your day, create highly predictable patterns, and sometimes try to control other people. Even your spiritual beliefs or worldview may leave little room for mystery or ambiguity. Sometimes I self-medicate by controlling my physical world. Organizing my possessions is one way I try to control my unorganized feelings.

Food. You snack, binge, purge, or eat in excess. You use food to adjust your body chemistry when you're feeling lonely, restless, and vulnerable. During one stressful season of life, I'd park outside a local bakery and eat a small banana cream pie . . . by myself . . . in the car . . . every week. I called it "self-care," but it was actually unhealthy self-indulgence.

Sex. You compulsively pleasure yourself, have one-night stands, engage in risky sex, or look at pornography. Like with food, you use arousal and orgasm to manipulate your body chemistry to provide temporary relief from stress and anxiety. It's easier to settle for a rush of adrenaline and hormones than to do the healthier work of facing our anxiety.

Alcohol. You drink regularly and minimize how important drinking is to you, or you have a dependency on alcohol. The fact that alcohol is a depressant complicates your anxiety. Personally, I've never developed a taste for alcohol. Someone once accused me of being a "prudish teetotaler." I replied, "I'm not against alcohol. I have other addictions—I don't need another one."

Drugs. You use nicotine or illicit drugs. Maybe you have continued taking prescribed pain medications for a past injury because they make you feel better emotionally. This is self-medicating. Let me clarify: I am not advising you to discontinue medications prescribed to help with legitimate pain from injuries or diagnosed mental health issues. Following a professional plan for wellness that includes medication is wise. But misuse of drugs is common.

Hoarding. You collect things you don't need, have difficulty getting rid of possessions, or have a problem with compulsive spending. Purchasing, obtaining, or not discarding possessions can light up pleasure centers in your brain associated with safety, security, and belonging. It's not uncommon to find a link between hoarding and ungrieved losses or traumatic events.

Body-focused repetitive behaviors (BFRBs). You scratch, pick your skin, pull or chew hair, or unconsciously bite your nails. Unlike more serious forms of self-injury, like cutting, you're not trying to hurt yourself, but you do. I've already mentioned that cheek biting is self-soothing activity that I am trying to unlearn.

Excessive self-examination. You read every book on anxiety, explore every website, spend hours thinking about your struggles with anxiety, or recruit a legion of helpers (therapists, pastors, friends, and mentors) to assist you in examining all aspects of your chronic worry, intrusive thoughts, and unwanted feelings. A healthy amount of self-examination is good for the soul, but too much can be another (and ironic!) form of avoidance.

We all self-soothe and self-medicate. Most of what we use to self-medicate isn't bad in and of itself. It works for a while, which is why we need to recognize its danger. The good news is we don't need to self-medicate anymore. We can identify and begin to reduce our self-medicating habits.

ACTION STEPS

1. *Make a list of self-medicating behaviors you can reduce.* Look back on your most recent or intense times of anxiety. What behaviors did you engage in to try to avoid, extinguish, or numb yourself to your thoughts and feelings? How could you use an *Anxiety Field Guide* skill instead? Try this the next time you are anxious.

2. *Brainstorm some healthy ways to self-soothe.* What are some healthy activities you can do to reduce stress and find rest? Begin doing these activities while reducing your self-medicating behaviors. You may feel stress and anxiety as you reduce your unhealthy self-medicating. This is normal. Give yourself grace and keep moving toward making healthy decisions.

3. *Get help for your addictions, compulsions, and mental wellness issues.* There are many new and helpful treatment approaches for times when we find ourselves stuck in our hurts, habits, and hang-ups. If you have an underlying struggle that is feeding your anxiety, please be courageously vulnerable and get support. This can come through professional counseling, a recovery program, a support group, or medical help.

26

Create New Pathways

Anxiety operates from old neuropathways
in your brain. You can take control
of your thoughts and feelings by creating
new pathways for your brain to follow.

I **NORMALLY GO TO THE STORE** to buy my clothes. There is something comforting to me about having all my size and style options within reach of a dressing room. But I recently decided to shop online for some clothes. As I was searching online, I ran across a great-looking vest. I decided to venture out of my standard shirt and pants combo. I clicked to purchase it, and it arrived the next week. Done . . . or so I thought.

Over the following weeks, I was bombarded with ads for vests from every company imaginable and on every digital platform available. Emails, social media posts, and mailers flooded my inbox. By saying yes to that one purchase, I got more than I ever wanted. It took me quite a while to stop the flood of unsolicited ads and requests.

The reason I was flooded with ads was because of a complex computer algorithm designed by coders to track users' preferences and purchases to market more consumer products. When you view, search, or purchase something online, a program notes it and then offers suggestions of similar products you might like. In one way, the algorithm is trying to help focus and clarify your interests. At the same time, it is narrowing your perspective of the world to see only what you have chosen in the past.

Our brains work in a similar way.

Like these complex algorithms, God designed our brains to always be making connections between past experiences, emotional responses, and future decisions. For example, my son touched a hot stovetop when he was little. It burned his fingers. His brain made a connection between hot stovetops and pain. Now, whenever he goes to touch a hot stove, his brain remembers and sends mental, biological, and emotional cues telling him to be careful. These come through what are called *neural pathways* in his brain. This is good!

Here's another example. When my wife, Marie, was a young girl, she had a deep desire to be known, loved, and protected. She was also innocent and trusting. Throughout her childhood years, when she attempted to trust those closest to her, she was often neglected, rejected, or abused. Her brain remembered. For much of her adulthood, when a trusting relationship began to form, an automatic (and often unconscious) wall of protection formed in her—even when there was nothing to fear. The neuropathways in her brain were connecting past experiences and emotional responses with her present decisions. This was not good.

Becoming aware of the coded algorithms online and taking steps to change them is similar to allowing God to begin creating new neural pathways in us related to anxiety.

When you're worried, your brain wants to help you. It wants to confirm your worry, so it'll scan your past experiences in which worries were valid and look for negative stories from your past that are tagged with hurt. These thoughts, feelings, and memories then flood your conscious mind and trigger physiological reactions in your body. The message you get is, *You should be worried.* But this message might not be accurate at all. Going back to the example of shopping for a vest, the message the ads sent me was, "You love vests! You probably want to see more." The algorithm was doing its job, but it was wrong. I don't love vests and didn't want more!

Your brain operates similarly when you're not worried. I sat down to watch a movie recently, and the opening logo for the production company appeared on the screen. The beginning chords of the beautiful orchestral score filled the room. Without thinking, I immediately lay back comfortably in my seat, and everything I'd been ruminating about that day exited my mind. My brain found all kinds of past experiences, feelings, and good thoughts associated with movie watching. My brain remembered and sent me the message, *You like this. You can relax. This is going to be a good experience.* And it was.

Our brains like to find similarities and create patterns so that decisions can be made quickly. My friend Chris described these "neural pathways" to me with a story from the beach. He said, "I took my kids to the beach, and they built a small little mountain of sand. Then they got a cup of water from the ocean and poured it on the top of the little mountain. It poured down the side and created a little pathway. Then they decided to do it again. They got another cup of water and poured it on the top of the little mountain." He then asked me, "Guess what it did?"

I said, "It created another little pathway?"

"No," he replied, "the water found the easiest way down the mountain. It used the pathway that was already there—and that's how our brains work."

Have you ever noticed that it's easier to have good thoughts and feelings when you are having a good day? And that when you are having a bad day, it's hard to snap out of it? That's because your brain is always looking for the easiest and quickest pattern. When you're having a good day, your brain helps you continue to have a good day. When you are having a bad day, your brain helps you continue to have a bad day.

Sometimes a very strong unwanted thought or feeling can trigger your brain to find a familiar "worry pathway." This happened to me this morning. I was having a good conversation with my son Ethan. I was relaxed, with no plans for the afternoon, and we were laughing about a joke. It was a good day. Then, a word was said, and everything changed. I can't even remember what the word was, but my brain linked it to some past worry and *boom!* I was triggered and all these anxious feelings flooded me. My brain interrupted my time with my son like an unwanted guest sharing an unrelated story.

In that moment, I had a choice. I decided to "reroute the water of my thinking" toward something more positive. I took a deep breath, adjusted the seat cushion beneath me (grounding), and gently directed my attention back to the conversation with my son. It worked. I didn't have to follow that pathway of worry and negativity.

God has designed our brains with "neuroplasticity." That means we can change our old neural pathways of worry, avoidance, rumination, ritual, and greater anxiety. We can create new pathways of awareness, mindfulness, exposure, healthy response, and peace.

ACTION STEPS

1. *Ask God to help you begin changing old and unhealthy pathways in your thinking and feeling.* You've been doing this already by slowing down, becoming aware of yourself, and using a mood log. Now ask God to help you be more intentional in creating new patterns of thinking and feeling.

2. *Create a visual timeline of your neuropathways.* Draw a horizontal line and divide it into four equal segments. In the first segment, write a regular intrusive thought or feeling you experience. In the second segment write the internal message or negative voice that reinforces that thought or feeling for you. In the third segment, write your normal but unhealthy response to this (avoidance, negative self-talk, or compulsion). In the fourth segment, record how intense the unwanted thought or feeling is. After you have done this, use the skills you've

learned to create a new timeline for each of your experiences. I've included an example of this at the end of the chapter.

3. *Rank your positivity.* On a scale of one to ten, how positive are you? In what situations and with which people do you tend to be more naturally positive? What contributes to your negativity? What practices could you put into place to help you have a generally more positive outlook on life? Remember, when you are positive, your brain will help you remain positive. When you are negative, your brain will help you stay negative.

Table 26.1. Old neuropathway timeline

UNWANTED THOUGHT/FEELING:	INTERNAL MESSAGE/ NEGATIVE VOICE:	UNHEALTHY RESPONSES:	INTENSITY LEVEL:
"I think or feel like I did something wrong."	"You made a mistake again!"	ruminating on the negative	On a scale of 1-10: 8
	"You can't fail."	reassurance seeking	
	"What will people think?"	avoiding my feelings self-medicating	

Table 26.2. New neuropathway timeline

UNWANTED THOUGHT/FEELING:	INTERNAL MESSAGE/ POSITIVE VOICE:	HEALTHY RESPONSES:	INTENSITY LEVEL:
"I think or feel like I did something wrong."	"Maybe I did, maybe I didn't."	Thank God for my feelings.	On a scale of 1-10: 4!
	"Mistakes are normal."	Observe before owning.	That's progress!
	"I can learn from this."	Practice grounding exercises.	
	"I have people who love and accept me."	Reach out for support.	

27

Adapt to Changes in Your Leadership

More responsibility can lead to more anxiety.
You can learn new ways to respond to changes
in your influence and leadership.

W E WERE IN THE MIDDLE of a major reorganization at work. We were about to make big decisions that would affect people's lives. I was the guy in charge, and I'd never had this level of responsibility.

I couldn't focus. I couldn't sleep. I found myself pacing around my house in the middle of the night. I was exhausted. I tried reading, praying, exercising, and cleaning the house. Nothing was helping my anxiety. I remember thinking to myself, *Where are the "grownups" around here? How did I end up with this kind of influence? How can I be a good leader if I have so much anxiety?*

I decided to distract myself by watching some videos online. While searching my options, I found a commercial for an outdoor company. It was a montage of different athletes doing extreme sports like wingsuit flying, cave diving, and motocross. The last athlete they showed was a mountain climber wearing an oxygen tank. That climber only appeared for a second, but the image stuck with me.

I quickly searched for articles on mountain climbers with oxygen tanks and learned more about what is called *altitude sickness*. As climbers go higher and higher, the air has less oxygen. Symptoms of altitude sickness include nausea, fatigue, lethargy, disoriented thinking, and difficulty sleeping. I thought, *That's what's happening to me! I'm climbing the mountain of leadership and it's making me sick!*

With leadership comes anxiety.

You might be thinking to yourself, "But I'm not a leader." Actually, you are. Leadership is about influence. You are an influencer in your family, with friends, at school or work, and in your community. You may not have a formal leadership role in these places, but your words, actions, and presence can shape the lives of other people.

Increases in leadership increase anxiety.

You get a promotion at work, are chosen to lead a group project at school, become a new parent, or start caring for an aging parent. Sometimes a crisis can thrust us into a position of leadership. This can lead to what's called *responsibility anxiety*.

Climbers who don't adapt to changes in altitude don't finish the climb. Like the mountain climbers, if we don't acclimate properly to increases in our leadership, our long-term influence will be negatively affected. Our "altitude sickness" can cause us to become defensive, protective, overly rigid in strategic decisions, too passive, or too dictatorial. Left untreated, this can lead to forms of leadership sabotage like burnout and moral failure. You may have experienced this already, or you may be sensing it could be in your future.

To acclimate to changes in altitude, seasoned climbers stop at base camps. These are staging areas where climbers ready themselves for the next elevation. We have similar base camps to manage our responsibility anxiety and practice healthy self-leadership.

Base Camp 1: Delegation. Anxiety grows as we carry responsibilities that are not ours to carry. Those of us with chronic worry, intrusive thoughts, and unwanted feelings usually have excessive feelings of personal responsibility. We feel like we're not doing enough. We believe success and failure rest on us. We don't want to let people down. We need to learn to distinguish what belongs to us and what belongs to others.

Setting personal boundaries and giving away responsibility is tough. We're afraid people will think we're being selfish. But delegation is not just offloading responsibility onto others so we can feel healthier. It's about empowering others to contribute their best, working as a team for a shared victory. Anxiety says, "I can get there on my own." Delegation says, "We can go further together."

Base Camp 2: Energy management. Anxiety grows when we're depleted, pressured, and joyless. Our anxiety drives us to work harder, not smarter. This leads us to focus on time management. We fear we won't have enough time, focus on what's not done, and worry about when we'll be able to finish. Energy management is about learning our natural strengths and rhythms within the time we've been given to work smarter, not harder.

Fear will drive us far beyond our capacity to be successful. There is a point when more input leads to less output. This is called the "law of diminishing returns." Good self-leadership means planning for energy, not just time. We must manage our energy so we can have the success we want. Anxiety asks, "Can't you do more . . . now?" Energy management asks, "When is the best time to do this, and for how long?"

Base Camp 3: Quicker decision making. Leadership is all about making decisions without all the information. We are used to over-thinking our decisions. This is because we have an underdeveloped view of failure. We believe success comes from not failing—but that's not true. Success comes from failing enough times to discover what works. The greater our leadership influence, the quicker our decisions must be made.

Of course, quick decisions can be bad decisions, but when you're a leader, a bad decision is sometimes better than no decision. Anxiety says, "I'm not sure this will work, so let's not do it." Quicker decision making says, "Let's give it a try and learn from it."

ACTION STEPS

1. *Make your schedule work for you.* Think about your average day and answer these questions: Are you a morning person or evening person? At what time of day are you most creative, making good decisions, and most ready to handle menial tasks? How far in advance do you need to think before acting? Which days, weeks, and seasons of the year are you most productive? Make a few small changes to your schedule to align with your natural energy rhythms. Your fear ladder and mood log might provide some helpful information on this.

2. *Give away responsibility.* Think about your relationships at home, school, work, and other areas of your life. Are you doing too much? Choose one responsibility you could ask someone else to do. If the idea of giving away responsibility gives you anxiety, that's a good indication that you should do it. Trust yourself—your high sense of responsibility probably means you'll hand it off to the right person. It's not their competence that's preventing you, it's your anxiety. Choose something simple. Give it a try and see what happens.

3. *Increase your decision-making speed.* Identify a decision that you have been delaying making, and then make the decision. After the decision is made, make some notes about your thoughts and feelings before, during, and after you made the decision. Try to sense what you need to make decisions more quickly. When I did this, I realized I like to have a long "decision runway." If possible, I do better with more time to think before I decide. But I can also get lost in my own head. My team has also told me, "Don't ruminate alone. Let us be a part of it." I'm learning to decide with others more often.

28

You Can Do It!

Anxiety can feel like strong waves threatening to pull us underwater. Instead of focusing on the waves, we can focus on the One who has power over the waves.

JESUS AND HIS DISCIPLES had just finished a long day of teaching and caring for people. He even performed one of his most well-known miracles—feeding five thousand people with only a small portion of food. Jesus told his disciples to go home ahead of him. So they got into a boat to head to the other side of a lake as Jesus went off by himself to pray.

As the sun set and they were far out into the lake, a huge storm hit. Their last memory of a storm on that sea had been with Jesus. During that storm, he had miraculously calmed the waves. This time, he was nowhere in sight.

In the middle of the night, the disciples saw a strange image in the distance. It was the figure of someone walking along the waves. They wondered if it was a ghost. Maybe the storm had killed one of them and this was his spirit greeting them from the great beyond. Or maybe the storm had killed all of them and this was the angel of death coming for them!

As the figure approached the boat, a familiar voice called out, "Don't be afraid." It was Jesus! Or so they thought.

One of the disciples, Peter, wanted to know for sure. In his boldness he called out to the ghostly figure, "If it is you, Jesus, let me come to you on the water!"

The voice responded, "Come."

Peter climbed over the side of the boat, just as he had done many times to pull in his fishing nets. This time, his feet didn't go under the water. Instead, he found himself standing on the waves as if on solid ground. It was Jesus! Peter made eye contact with him and began to walk toward him on the water! His joy was greater than his fear.

But then something caused him to stop looking at Jesus. Perhaps it was a sudden gust of cold air that distracted him. Peter suddenly realized that he was defying the laws of nature by walking on water. Right at that moment, he began to sink. As he sank beneath the waves, he shouted, "Lord, save me!" Immediately he felt the strong grip of Jesus pull him out of the water, and they got into the boat together.

Then Jesus asked him, "Why did you doubt?"

Great question.

Bodies of water in the Bible are often associated with danger, mystery, and peril. The Bible starts with the earth covered in water—formless and void—and continues with Noah's flood, the Red Sea that swallowed the Egyptians, uncontrollable sea creatures described by Job, a huge fish that engulfed Jonah, and stormy shipwrecks in the New Testament. Even the apostle John's apocalyptic vision of heaven has a river flowing from the throne of God, but no sea!

Unlike the Vikings, the ancient Hebrews were not a seafaring people. Even though Jesus' disciple Peter was a fisherman by vocation, he was smart enough to not step into the water during a violent storm. So why did he do it? How did he do it? What does it take to step out into a place that's unstable, unpredictable, and uncertain?

It takes faith.

Faith is relying on what we believe, not on what we see. Peter had seen Jesus' power over sickness, incurable diseases, demon possession, and religious authorities. But inviting Peter to walk on water? This was different. Peter's faith was not in his knowledge of the water but in what Jesus was inviting him to do.

Jesus didn't just give Peter permission. He gave Peter power—not just approval, but ability. Jesus never asks us to do something that he doesn't also equip us to do! And what empowered Peter was his relationship with Jesus. When Jesus said, "Come," he was telling Peter, "With me, you can do it." This explains what happened next.

When Peter's attention shifted away from Jesus, he began to sink. Losing his focus caused him to think about his problem more than his master. In doing this, Peter gave more control to the storm, and he almost went under. We can't blame him. He was exhausted from keeping his boat afloat all night. Fatigue often threatens one's ability to focus.

But all was not lost. Peter's focus shifted elsewhere, but Jesus' did not. As always, Jesus was there and ready to help. In the unpredictable, dangerous, and perilous threats of the unknown, Jesus took control and proved himself faithful to Peter. He does the same with us.

Anxiety is a lot like those violent waves. Sometimes Jesus miraculously calms them, but most of the time, he invites us to walk on them. Having faith doesn't eliminate discomfort, problems, or perceived threats. Faith keeps us focused on Jesus when we're overwhelmed by our thoughts and feelings. The more attention we give our anxiety, the more likely it is to pull us under.

Years ago, my son Ethan and I went to a camp in Northern California called JH Ranch. It's designed to help parents and teenagers form stronger bonds through adventure. One day, a group of us fathers and sons did a high-ropes course that was fifty feet in the air. We were strapped onto safety wires, and our sons had to walk backward on a tightrope while leading the fathers forward. Ethan is very athletic and has great balance. He made his way out backward and then told me to step out to meet him. The instant I stepped onto the rope, it started wobbling. I freaked out. The more I looked at the rope under my feet, the more I tried to counterbalance, making it wobble even more.

Then my son, in an authoritative voice, said, "Dad. Look at me. Don't look at the rope. Watch me. You can do it." I did what he said. I was scared and overthinking it, but we made it! What helped me the most was paying attention to my son, not the ropes—him, not me; his voice, not the anxious voices in my head.

This is the lesson of Peter walking on the water: Keeping our eyes on Jesus is the way forward. When we are tired, scared, and feel like we are sinking, we can reach out and find his firm grip, reminding us that we are loved and not alone.

ACTION STEPS

1. *What is your boat?* What is that place of safety and security Jesus is inviting you to step out of to move closer to him? Maybe you are secure in your career and Jesus is inviting you into another line of work. Maybe you feel stable in your schedule and Jesus is asking you to start something new. Perhaps your current level of anxiety is comfortable, and Jesus wants you to take another step of exposure.

2. *What is your storm?* What is most likely to pull your attention away from the steps of faith Jesus is inviting you to take? Other people's opinions? Concerns about money? Fear of the unknown? Self-defeating voices in your head? The possibility of embarrassment? Memories of past traumas or failures?

3. *How can you stay focused on Jesus?* What practical changes can you make in your behaviors and schedule to keep your eyes on Jesus? Limit your focus on the negative? Take spiritual breaks throughout the day? Change how you process email or social media? Read the Bible daily? Maintain regular involvement with your faith community?

29

Go for the Grit Award

Anxiety awakens your fear of failure.
Learn to see struggles as opportunities
for personal growth and greater resilience.

M Y OLDER SON, ASA, knew at an early age that he had the mind of an engineer. We were excited when he got into a high school built around STEM curriculum (science, technology, engineering, and mathematics). It had a fabrication lab, professional mentors, and a thriving robotics team. Intelligent and driven, he looked forward to his school's annual student awards. He was recognized that night with what they called the "Grit Award."

Here's how they described it:

> Grit Awards go to students who pushed themselves beyond the expectations to take on new challenges, students who looked for opportunities to move forward when they could have stepped back without consequence, or students who were struggling and continued to persevere by attending office hours, asking questions in class, or just having a positive attitude toward what they were learning.

My son was kind of disappointed. He hoped to have the best GPA, get on the honor roll, or receive something that recognized his intellectual and academic achievement.

We often want to measure ourselves by objective standards. We rank our value or achievement by comparing ourselves to the external accomplishments of others. We judge ourselves on whether we got the A, got first place, or beat the high score. Our culture rewards those who cross the finish line first. As a result, many people don't recognize the character qualities that lead to success—qualities like self-control, forbearance, faithfulness, goodness, and joy. I believe there's a better way to evaluate ourselves: Do we have "grit"?

The word *grit* comes from an Old Saxon word that refers to pebbles or gravel. It's a word picture for someone who is tough and able to endure. People with grit know that comfort is the enemy of growth. They are always taking new ground; they are pioneers who never settle and who see hardship as the pathway to lasting success.

Grit is about firmness of mind. It's the determination to keep going, even when the end is not in sight. It's about finding the pleasure in running the race just as much as finishing it. It's a toughness of spirit, unswayed by the dubious messages of emotion and past failure. It's the ability to see that transformation comes more often through our losses than our wins.

When it comes to dealing with anxiety, go for the Grit Award.

You're almost done with this book because you have grit! Let's go through the description of the Grit Award and see how it applies to you.

You are taking on new challenges. You're much more aware of your anxiety than you were when you started. You've decided to not accept the control that it has over you. You're starting to recognize intrusive thoughts and unwanted feelings for what they are—your brain's attempt to protect you from harm or unhelpful leftover messages from your past. Some of these internal messages' origins and purposes are unexplainable. You have decided to not panic. You are reminding yourself that your feelings don't define you. You're also trying new skills to be healthy. This isn't easy, but you are doing it!

You are moving forward when you could step back. You could have put the book down already. In fact, you probably have. Maybe multiple times! That's okay, because you are here now and you're starting to see things differently. You probably have some (or many) of your old behaviors and habits. You're still tempted to give in to your old way of thinking. But you're headed in the right direction. Hopefully, this book is changing you. Even trying some of the principles in this book just once has begun altering your brain chemistry for the better. You might be moving slower than you'd like, but you're making progress. You are doing it!

You are persevering to stay positive. You have anxiety because you don't see things happening the way you believe they should. You want the best and believe the best. You are a person of hope. Over the years, your brain has learned to see more negative than positive. Now you know that God has another plan for you. You are working to be hopeful, faithful, and forward-looking. You are becoming more emotionally resilient—not allowing unwanted feelings to paralyze you. Some of this book has been stressful and challenging, but you've kept going.

What's important to remember is that we all make progress in different ways and at different speeds. Some of you are beginning to see some movement in a good direction, and others of you have already had major breakthroughs. What's important is that you are doing the work. This is why you get the Grit Award!

The Grit Award is *not* about what you've accomplished; it's about who you are. If you look back on the titles of each of the chapters in this book, you'll see that I've tried to write each one in the present tense. This was intentional. These are not a checklist of items to complete, but invitations to ongoing practices for people with grit.

I have a friend who is an athletic beast. He competes in triathlons. He invited me to one of them (as a spectator, that is). I spent the day hanging out with the friends and family member of other triathletes while he swam, biked, and ran. As all the runners began to make their way to the finish line at their different speeds, I heard a strange noise. It was the sound of cowbells!

There's a tradition of ringing cowbells at the end of a race as a symbolic way of encouraging tired runners to keep going. I found a small merchandise table selling cowbells, bought one, and watched for my friend. As he came by, I rang my heart out! I was so proud of him, not for winning or placing at a certain level, but for working so hard, being patient with himself, getting up when he had fallen down, and having the self-discipline to keep going when everything inside of him was saying "give up."

You might be feeling some of those things.

Here's what I want you to know: I'm ringing the bell for you.

ACTION STEPS

1. *See challenges as opportunities for growth.* Make a short list of the biggest challenges you are facing. Rewrite each challenge as an opportunity. For example, "I have to face that controlling family member" can become "I have the opportunity to be myself in a strong and a loving way." Life is about growth, and growth only comes through challenges.

2. *Guard against measuring yourself by external objective accomplishments.* You can't avoid objective standards like grades, deadlines, and balance sheets. But instead of measuring yourself against the aggregated successes of others, look at each situation as an opportunity to let God's Spirit work in and through you. Galatians 5:22-23 contains a list of ways in which the Holy Spirit wants to show himself in our character. Take time to look over this passage and look for ways to grow in "fruitfulness."

3. *Learn to get up quickly after a fall.* You are going to miss opportunities and make choices that will feel disastrous. Get back up and keep going. Proverbs 24:16 says, "The godly may trip seven times, but they will get up again." Don't measure your success by how many times you make mistakes but by how you recover from them.

30

Believe the Good News

Religion can stir up your anxiety
by making you believe that your relationship
with God is up to you, but God
has a cure for spiritual anxiety.

WASN'T RAISED IN A PARTICULARLY RELIGIOUS HOME. My first significant experience with faith was when I was invited to a summer program for kids at a church in my neighborhood. There were games, costumes from Bible stories, and a mandatory chapel service to attend. As a kid, I was bored to death sitting through those chapel services. Religion didn't make much sense to me.

My next significant moment of faith happened when my dad was sick. It's the first time I remember praying. I said, "God, if you exist, please heal my dad. If you do, I'll give you my life and do whatever you want." My dad died a year and a half later. I thought, *Well, that's no use.* I wouldn't pray again for almost a decade.

In high school, I had my first religious experience. It happened late one night in my girlfriend's bedroom of all places! She left the room at one point, and as she closed the door, I saw a crucifix on her wall. I immediately felt religious guilt. A message came to my mind saying, "Jason, that's my daughter." Yikes! I wasn't even a person of faith, but suddenly I felt like I'd offended God!

My life changed in the most profound way in college. Believing I'd missed out on a huge area of study—religious education—I enrolled in a philosophy of religion class. One afternoon as I was waiting for that class to begin, I looked at the green grass and the blue sky. I was strangely captured by their beauty. In that moment, I experienced an unsolicited conviction that there was something responsible for all the beauty I was seeing.

That experience started me on a spiritual search to find this mysterious being with whom I'd played a form of spiritual "tag" over the years. I started with very creation-centered spiritualities. I looked into Greenpeace, Earth-based religions, and naturalistic philosophy, but none of them seemed to resonate with the very personal experience I'd had. I eventually found myself in a very unlikely place—a small African American church in South Central Los Angeles. Behind barred windows, people sang, played tambourines, and talked about Jesus like they knew him personally! Here I heard the good news of God's love for me and found an answer for my spiritual searching.

What does this have to do with anxiety?

Are you ever worried about "being right with God" or worried that you are not forgiven for things you've done wrong? Do you ever get concerned that you're not good enough to get into heaven (if there is one)? Maybe you get religious worries and then quickly try to dismiss them, ignore them, or rationalize them away.

Many people have some form of spiritual or religious anxiety.

Some even suffer from a form of obsessive-compulsive disorder called *scrupulosity*. Scrupulosity is when people turn spiritual expressions of love and devotion to God into compulsions to ease their anxiety. They may be excessively concerned about avoiding things that would lead them or others to sin. They memorize the Bible or make pacts and promises with God to secure spiritual protection, or they overindulge in cleansing rituals (like confession, purity prayers, or deliverance prayers) to rid themselves of spiritual impurity. They may obsessively fixate on specific areas of theology like predeterminism, spiritual warfare, or the end times.

When our spirituality and anxiety overlap, we can gently remind ourselves that God's good news for us is greater than our anxiety. Here's how I'd summarize this good news that was shared with me.

You are an important part of God's good creation. God has made this beautiful world, and you hold a special place in it. You are made in the image of God. This means you have honor, dignity, abilities, and a degree of power unlike anything else in creation. It's not because of anything you have done or not done. You are valuable because you have been created by God's love. And that same Creator desires a personal relationship with you. Having a relationship with your Creator can help you with your anxiety, find purpose in this life, and experience fullness in the life to come.

You are part of a world that is out of sync with God. While there is a lot of good around us, the world is not operating as God planned. Suffering, brokenness, and injustice remind us of this. And with God's gift of free will come our bad choices. The old story of Adam and Eve is a memorial and example of how we human beings, left to ourselves, can go our own way. By instinct and choice, we move away from God. Jesus called this "sin." It's like a spiritual sickness that causes us to be both "sinners" and the "sinned against." Fortunately, there is hope!

We have been fought for and sought after. All the years of spiritual longing in human beings have led to an amazing event—God entering his own creation in the person of Jesus. When Jesus died on the cross, he was showing you God's selfless love; paying the debt for the wrongs you've done; and taking all the evil, injustice, and brokenness of the world onto himself, extinguishing their power, and opening a door to forgiveness and hope. Jesus is the finale to God's great story of humanity. Through his resurrection, he ushers in a new way of life and a new kingdom we can belong to now.

We are invited to be part of God's new creation. We can stop restlessly trying to be more religious, making sure we're "sorry enough" about our sins, or trying to do enough good works to outweigh our bad works. God invites us to be part of the perfect new world Jesus is creating. Here's the ironic twist—the way to new life is through our imperfection. New life with Jesus is an invitation to embrace God, not certainty; faith, not predictability; and rest, not perfectionism. It's when we can take our religious-themed anxiety and let God graciously sit with us rather than begging God to make it go away.

The people in Jesus' day suffered from religious anxiety. Like a heavy wooden yoke on the shoulders of oxen plowing the fields, their "yokes" were guilt, shame, religious duty, and feelings of distance from God. They felt like they were not good enough. But Jesus, in his love, had a life-giving invitation to those burdened with religious anxiety. It's also an invitation for us.

He said, "Come to me, all of you who are weary and carry heavy burdens, and I will give you rest. Take my yoke upon you. Let me teach you, because I am humble and gentle at heart, and you will find rest for your souls. For my yoke is easy to bear, and the burden I give you is light" (Matthew 11:28-30).

This is good news!

ACTION STEPS

1. *Say yes to the good news!* Try a simple prayer like this: "God, I believe you made me and love me. I am a flawed and broken person. Thank you for sending Jesus to die and rise again. Forgive me for my sins. I give you the leadership of my life. Thank you for your love for me and helping me thrive as a new creation in you." Find someone you can tell about this decision you've made.

2. *Find your identity in God's love for you, not your religious anxiety.* Our actions flow from our identity, not the other way

around. Try reading this enlightening part of a letter in the New Testament: Ephesians 1:1-14. There are around twenty different descriptions of what it means to be in a relationship with God (for example, forgiven, chosen, adopted). See how many you can find! Which ones resonate most with you? How can these help you when you feel anxiety?

Final Thoughts

TWO YEARS AGO, I found a hobby that helped me with my anxiety. I create handheld crosses made from salvaged metal and broken clock parts. I go to estate sales on weekends to look for supplies. When an old tinkerer passes away and leaves a garage full of rusted nuts, bolts, and unknown scrap metal—that's when I come alive! I like the stuff no one else wants.

I call them redeemed crosses. The word *redeem* means to restore, win back, or exchange for something better. The idea behind these crosses is that God has a way of taking the broken, discarded, and unwanted things in our lives and making something beautiful.

Every cross I make is unique. Each one looks different and takes a different length of time to become what I want it to be. The crosses are also imperfect. Each one has scratches and flaws because they've seen wear and tear. Their imperfection is a reminder that perfection is reserved for the Divine.

The crosses I make are reminders of my journey with anxiety. I am unique and imperfect. I am learning to embrace these qualities in myself. I invite you to embrace them as well.

You are Unique and Imperfect

You are unique. Your struggles with anxiety may make you feel alone and different from others. Instead of seeing yourself as alone or different, try using the word *unique.* The word means one of a kind, like no one else. Your uniqueness gives you the opportunity to be yourself and to find out how to be the best version of yourself.

There's an old Jewish fable of a man who grew up going to synagogue hearing of the great leader Moses. From his childhood, he wanted to be like Moses. He worked hard throughout his life to model his life after this renowned spiritual leader of the Hebrew people. When he died, he asked God, "I worked so hard to be just like Moses. Did I make you proud?"

God replied, "I didn't want you to be Moses; I wanted you to be you."

God is inviting us to be ourselves—even our best selves. This only comes when we say yes to Jesus and then allow his forgiveness, power, and love to be expressed through us. God has created each and every one of us to be his image bearers and have a unique place in the family of God.

When you feel the pressure to be more than you are, compare yourself to others, or condemn yourself for mistakes you've made, remind yourself that you are unique. You are loved and God is at work within you!

You are imperfect. Imperfection may be a four-letter word to you. Your struggles with anxiety have caused you to emphasize your unfinished and broken parts. Perfection is a terrible taskmaster. Perfection says, "Your weaknesses are bad, your mistakes will haunt you, and there is something profoundly wrong with you." These are lies.

Our weaknesses remind us that we need others. Our mistakes can help us graciously learn and grow. That feeling of wrongness is an invitation into a closer relationship with God, who loves us. Imperfection shouldn't just be accepted; it can be embraced.

When you feel the pressure to be perfect, leave that job to God. Take all that energy you are putting into saying things exactly the right way and doing things right the first time, and channel it into being honest and courageously vulnerable with others.

Let's decide to be "imperfectionists." Try seeing imperfection as a beautiful reminder that there is only one perfect person in the universe, and that person loves you just the way you are.

Here's one final suggestion for you.

Create Your Own Field Guide

As I mentioned in the beginning, this book was created from the notes and insights that were most helpful to me. These are the healthy habits that have transformed my life. But now it's your turn. Read, listen, collect ideas, and see what works for you. Make notes of what is helpful to you and keep it handy. Make your own field guide!

Whatever the content of your field guide, it should be rooted in the principles I shared with you in the introduction. Hopefully, they have become more a part of your life throughout our time together. Here they are again:

- Normalization: Accept that anxiety is natural but can become unhealthy.

- Exposure: Understand your fears and begin facing them rather than avoiding them.

- Habituation: Use new skills to become desensitized to your fears.

- Care: Discover healthy ways to experience God's love for you and others.

How are these playing out in your life? In what ways can you incorporate these principles into your daily, weekly, or yearly routines? Where have you seen progress in your anxious thoughts and feelings by embracing these principles? How can you celebrate that progress in healthy ways?

The Road Ahead . . .

"If you had one word to describe Jesus, what would it be?"

This is a question the late Dallas Willard asked of Bill Gaultiere. Dallas Willard was a professor of philosophy at the University of Southern California and an expert in epistemology and spirituality. Bill Gaultiere and his wife, Kristi, are psychologists in Southern California. They founded an organization that offers counseling, coaching, and retreats for leaders.

One word to describe Jesus? Bill thought to himself. Some of the words that came to his mind were, *Loving. Holy. Teacher. Healer.*

After a lengthy silence, Willard offered his word: "Relaxed."

In his blog post "A Simple Solution to Stress from Dallas Willard," Bill describes that *relaxed* is not a word he had considered. It's not a word I'd considered either—but it's a good one. Jesus was relaxed. This doesn't mean he was stoic, unemotional, and unrattled by his circumstances. Jesus experienced the full range of human emotions, lived with complicated relationships, and suffered greatly to courageously fulfill his life mission. But he did all this with a sense of inner peace and resolve that is best described as "relaxed."

How can we be "relaxed" like Jesus? My temptation is to create a "to do" list. The idea being that if I can master certain skills, I will be rid of my anxiety for good. But that's not realistic. And it's actually unbiblical!

Fear, anxiety, and uncertainty all have a place in God's plan for our lives, just not the central place. The healthy habits we've explored here are not designed to be self-help tips or quick fixes to extinguish our unwanted thoughts or feelings, but invitations to keep following Jesus.

Like that path to the waterfall, long-term healing from anxiety is a path others have discovered before us and also a path we must find for ourselves. You'll make mistakes, circle back, and try new things. When the path is unclear, I want to encourage you to keep listening.

You'll hear the continual, gracious, loving, courageous, and disciplined invitation to relax and thrive in uncertainty.

Thanks for taking this journey with me. I want to encourage you to recommend this book to someone you know who is struggling with chronic worry, intrusive thoughts, and unwanted feelings. You can help others to navigate their own path with what you're learning.

Let's finish by reminding ourselves of Jesus' words for anyone with worry:

> I tell you not to worry about everyday life—whether you have enough food and drink, or enough clothes to wear. Isn't life more than food, and your body more than clothing? Look at the birds. They don't plant or harvest or store food in barns, for your heavenly Father feeds them. And aren't you far more valuable to him than they are? Can all your worries add a single moment to your life?
>
> And why worry about your clothing? Look at the lilies of the field and how they grow. They don't work or make their clothing, yet Solomon in all his glory was not dressed as beautifully as they are. And if God cares so wonderfully for wildflowers that are here today and thrown into the fire tomorrow, he will certainly care for you. Why do you have so little faith?
>
> So don't worry about these things, saying, "What will we eat? What will we drink? What will we wear?" These things dominate the thoughts of unbelievers, but your heavenly Father already knows all your needs. Seek the Kingdom of God above all else, and live righteously, and he will give you everything you need.
>
> So don't worry about tomorrow, for tomorrow will bring its own worries. Today's trouble is enough for today. (Matthew 6:25-34)

Acknowledgments

T HANK YOU TO THE ENTIRE TEAM at InterVarsity Press, specifically Ethan McCarthy, Rachel Hastings, and Lori Neff, who held my hand and faithfully guided me through what was not only a highly professional process but a refreshingly spiritual one as well. You embraced this journey of mine with wisdom, grace, and patience. I am truly grateful.

A big shout out to Sean Morgan and my Cohort Dawgs. You were with me in my toughest times and helped me find my way in this new season of faith and ministry. Thanks for the time and space you gave me to debrief and process. Most of all, I'm so honored to be in the trenches with you.

Thank you to my late-night phone partners. Pastor Brady Boyd, your sage advice and kind heart got me through so many seasons of challenge. Thank you for opening your life to me. Scott Ridout of Converge, like a coach you pushed me to keep moving forward. Pastor Bill Ankerberg, my spiritual father, you were the transition pastor for our church but also for me. And David Harris, thank you for helping me see that I needed to take my healing journey to the next level.

Facing my anxiety converged with my new leadership position at Journey of Faith. My deep thanks, as well as contrite grief, for you who have been with me in my anxiety, whether you knew it or not. Many of you experienced me spinning out, oversharing, or white knuckling it. Thank you for being kind, honest, and allowing me to make amends when possible. A special thank you to the executive team and elders who came alongside me in my tough times and helped make this book possible for others.

Someone deserving of special thanks is Krista Reyna, the executive coordinator at Journey of Faith and one of my dearest ministry companions. Krista, you have the honor/burden of being with me on the mountaintops and in the valleys. I am eternally grateful for both your quiet, empathetic presence as well as your God-given and growing prophetic voice in my life.

To my family. My amazing mother, you taught me resilience, endurance, and self-acceptance. You have been and will always be a walking miracle. My wife, Marie, there is no earthly one above you. Thank you for being a patient guide and companion. And my children, thank you for your love as you watched and prayed for your father through many anxious times.

To you, reader friend, thanks for sharing in *The Anxiety Field Guide* with me. May you be helped and be a help to others.

Most of all . . . to my tender and courageous Jesus. You are my anchor, my hope, and my Savior in the dark nights. May your loving sacrifice help everyone find the lasting healing they desire. All things are from you and for you for all generations, for ever and ever. Amen.

Recommended Resources

THERE ARE SO MANY GREAT RESOURCES available for finding freedom from anxiety. These are ones that have been an important part of my journey. I hope some of these will help you as well.

Anxiety

Freedom from Anxious Thoughts and Feelings: A Two-Step Mindfulness Approach for Moving Beyond Fear and Worry by Scott Symington

Try Softer: A Fresh Approach to Move Us out of Anxiety, Stress, and Survival Mode—and into a Life of Connection and Joy by Aundi Kolber

You Are Not Your Brain: The 4-Step Solution for Changing Bad Habits, Ending Unhealthy Thinking, and Taking Control of Your Life by Jeffrey M. Schwartz

Anxious for Nothing: Finding Calm in a Chaotic World by Max Lucado

When Panic Attacks: The New, Drug-Free Anxiety Therapy That Can Change Your Life by David D. Burns

What to Do When You Worry Too Much: A Kid's Guide to Overcoming Anxiety by Dawn Huebner and Bonnie Matthews

Overthinking

Get Out of Your Head: Stopping the Spiral of Toxic Thoughts by Jennie Allen

Women Who Think Too Much: How to Break Free of Overthinking and Reclaim Your Life by Susan Nolen-Hoeksema and Sheryl Bernstein

Obsessive-Compulsive Disorder

Brain Lock: Free Yourself from Obsessive-Compulsive Behavior by Jeffrey M. Schwartz

Freedom from Obsessive-Compulsive Disorder: A Personalized Recovery Program for Living with Uncertainty by Jonathan Grayson

Can Christianity Cure Obsessive-Compulsive Disorder? A Psychiatrist Explores the Role of Faith in Treatment by Ian Osborn

Overcoming Unwanted Intrusive Thoughts: A CBT-Based Guide to Getting Over Frightening, Obsessive, or Disturbing Thoughts by Sally M. Winston and Martin N. Seif

Grief, Loss, and Trauma

Recovering from Losses in Life by H. Norman Wright

Necessary Losses by Judith Viorst

The Body Keeps the Score: Brain, Mind, and Body in the Healing of Trauma by Bessel van der Kolk

Healing the Wounded Heart: The Heartache of Sexual Abuse and the Hope of Transformation by Dan Allender

A Grief Observed by C.S. Lewis

Spirituality

Abba's Child: The Cry of the Heart for Intimate Belonging by Brennan Manning

Rhythms of Renewal: Trading Stress and Anxiety for a Life of Peace and Purpose by Rebekah Lyons

The Louder Song: Listening for Hope in the Midst of Lament by Aubrey Sampson

The Lord's Prayer: A Guide to Praying to Our Father by Wesley Hill

Finding Quiet: My Story of Overcoming Anxiety and the Practices That Brought Peace by J. P. Moreland

Devotional Reading

Grace for the Moment: Inspirational Thoughts for Each Day of the Year by Max Lucado

Keep a Quiet Heart by Elisabeth Elliot

Through the Bible, Through the Year: Daily Reflections from Genesis to Revelation by John Stott

Unforced Rhythms: Why Daily Devotions Aren't for All of Us by Gwen Jackson

Personal Leadership

Speak Life: Restoring Healthy Communication in How You Think, Talk, and Pray by Brady Boyd

The Gifts of Imperfection: Let Go of Who You Think You're Supposed to Be and Embrace Who You Are by Brené Brown

Decisive: How to Make Better Choices in Life and Work by Chip Heath and Dan Heath

Mastering Fear: A Navy SEAL's Guide by Brandon Webb and John David Mann.

Leadership Pain: The Classroom for Growth by Samuel Chand and Tim Lundeen

The Wise Advocate: The Inner Voice of Strategic Leadership by Art Kleiner, Jeffrey Schwartz, and Josie Thomson

Managing Leadership Anxiety: Yours and Theirs by Steve Cuss

Relationships

Boundaries: When to Say Yes, How to Say No to Take Control of Your Life by John Townsend and Henry Cloud

The Seven Desires of Every Heart by Mark Laaser and Debra Laaser

How We Love by Milan Yerkovich and Kay Yerkovich

People Fuel: Fill Your Tank for Life, Love, and Leadership by John Townsend

Difficult Conversations: How to Discuss What Matters Most by Douglas Stone, Bruce Patton, and Sheila Heen

Index of Tools and Practices